GOVERNMENTS AS INTEREST GROUPS

GOVERNMENTS AS INTEREST GROUPS

Intergovernmental Lobbying and the Federal System

ANNE MARIE CAMMISA

Westport, Connecticut
London

Library of Congress Cataloging-in-Publication Data

Cammisa, Anne Marie.
    Governments as interest groups : intergovernmental lobbying and
the federal system / Anne Marie Cammisa.
        p.   cm.
    Includes bibliographical references and index.
    ISBN 0–275–94962–1 (alk. paper)
    1. Federal government—United States.   2. Lobbying—United States.
3. Pressure groups—United States.   4. State governments—United
States.   5. Federal-city relations—United States.   I. Title.
JK325.C27   1995
320.8′0973—dc20   95–14428

British Library Cataloguing in Publication Data is available.

Library of Congress Catalog Card Number: 95–14428
ISBN: 0–275–94962–1

First published in 1995

Praeger Publishers, 88 Post Road West, Westport, CT 06881
An imprint of Greenwood Publishing Group, Inc.

Printed in the United States of America

The paper used in this book complies with the
Permanent Paper Standard issued by the National
Information Standards Organization (Z39.48–1984).

10 9 8 7 6 5 4 3 2 1

*To Kay Kay, who remembers a little girl
who wanted to be an author*

Contents

Tables

Abbreviations

ABC—The Act for Better Child Care
ABC Coalition—The Alliance for Better Child Care
AFDC—Aid to Families with Dependent Children
AFDC-UP—Aid to Families with Dependent Children-Unemployed Parent
AFSCME—American Federation of State, County and Municipal Employees
APWA—American Public Welfare Association
CDBG—Community Development Block Grant
CDF—Children's Defense Fund
CLPHA—Council of Large Public Housing Authorities
CWEP—Community Work Experience Program
EITC—Earned Income Tax Credit
FAP—Family Assistance Program
FHA—Federal Housing Administration
FmHA—Farmers Home Administration
FSA—Family Support Act
GAP—Grant Action Program
GROW—Greater Opportunities Through Work
GRS—General Revenue Sharing
HHS—Department of Health and Human Services
HOME—HOME Investment Partnerships
HOP—Housing Opportunity Program
HOPE—Homeownership Opportunities for People Everywhere
HUD—Department of Housing and Urban Development
JOBS—Job Opportunities and Basic Skills Program
JTPA—Job Training Partnership Act
LIHEAP—Low-Income Home Energy Assistance Program
LISC—Local Initiatives Support Corporation

MDRC—Manpower Demonstration Research Corporation
NACO—National Association of Counties
NAHA—National Affordable Housing Act
NAHRO—National Association of Housing Redevelopment Officials
NCDA—National Community Development Assocation
NCSL—National Conference of State Legislatures
NETWork—National Education and Training Work Program
NGA—National Governors' Association
NLC—National League of Cities
OBRA—Omnibus Budget and Reconciliation Act
SSBG—Social Services Block Grant
SSI—Supplemental Security Income
USCM—U.S. Conference of Mayors
WIN—Work Incentive Program

Preface

State and local governments emerged as important interest groups in response to increased federal grants in the 1960s. That decade witnessed a rapid expansion of federal social programs administered at the state and local levels, while the 1970s and 1980s were distinguished by attempts to give states and localities more responsibility over such programs. The current political environment is characterized by decreasing federal domestic spending, and the economic environment is characterized by concerns about federal, state and local debt. Changes in the political and economic environments may influence the system of federalism, and may have an impact on state and local interest groups' effectiveness at lobbying in the federal arena. This study examines the lobbying tactics and success of the five state and local lobbying groups (the National League of Cities, the U.S. Conference of Mayors, the National Association of Counties, the National Conference of State Legislatures and the National Governors' Association) during the late 1980s and early 1990s.

Many individuals provided assistance and support as I began and completed this work. First and foremost is Dr. William Gormley, my mentor at Georgetown University's Department of Government. Without his encouragement and advice, this book would not have been possible. His support over the years is greatly appreciated. Also at Georgetown University, Dr. Sue Thomas and Dr. Clyde Wilcox supplied encouragement and helpful suggestions. Dr. Walter Berns deserves special mention, because he taught me the art of critical thinking. The Department of Government at Suffolk University provided support during the final stages of the process, and my students there have been a source of motivation for completing this work. I owe a debt of gratitude to the American Political Science Association, whose Congressional Fellowship enabled me to see the process from the inside out rather than from the outside in. Also, I would like to thank the Henry A. Murray Research Center at

Radcliffe College, which appointed me a Visiting Scholar in 1994-1995 and provided me with resources and support. Special thanks also go to the many individuals who took the time to respond to my questions and provide their insights for this work. The congressional staff, interest group staff and gubernatorial staff that I interviewed were a source of rich information, and each respondent provided interesting perspectives on the legislative process. Since I promised them anonymity, I cannot mention names, but their cooperation was greatly appreciated

I owe a special thanks to my friends and co-workers at the Urban Institute. With them, I gained practical experience in evaluating public policies, and they have been a continuing source of friendship and moral support. Thank you, Demetra Nightingale, Pamela Holcomb, Carolyn O'Brien, Barbara Cohen, Sue Poppink, Regina Yudd, Kristin Seefeldt, Mildred Woodhouse and Sonya Drumgoole. Also, the late Lee Bawden is sorely missed; he possessed a rare combination of kindness and intellect which will always serve as a source of inspiration.

Thanks also go to my family, especially my parents, Guido and Mary Ida Cammisa, whose love and encouragement have been unwavering. My brothers Jim and Michael have always lent a hand when I needed it, and their support and patience is much appreciated. My gratitude also goes to my aunt, Katharine Thomas, who always had faith in me. Also in the category of family is my cousin, Laurie Cammisa, whose sense of humor has been an invaluable resource for me. Without my family, this book would not be here. Thanks also to Jacqueline Lee, for having confidence that I could complete this project.

Last but not least, I would like to thank my husband, Dr. Paul Christopher Manuel, whose undying optimism and love have helped me through graduate school, through my first years as a professor and through the process of completing this book. His dedication to his own work has been a constant source of inspiration for me. He has always been willing to listen, and I have gained countless insights from conversations with him. I owe a debt of gratitude to him that cannot be measured. Thanks to Paul and to all his family for their continued support, especially Joaquim and Barbara Manuel and Elvira Lagomarsino, and thanks to all the others who have helped me realize my goal.

Chapter I

The System of Federalism and the Policymaking Process

One of the defining features of American government is the system of federalism, which divides decision-making authority between the national (federal) government and the fifty state governments. The Constitution specifically grants power and authority to each level of government, although how that power should be divided is left vague. Article I, section 9 gives Congress the authority to make all laws "necessary and proper" for carrying out its powers. Article VI states that the Constitution and the laws and treaties that the national government makes under it constitute the "supreme law of the land." On the other hand, Amendment X reserves for the states any powers not specifically granted to the national government. In the early days of the Republic, the division of governmental authority did not present much of a problem: most of the action of governing was performed at the state and local levels. However, as the country matured, and the issues and problems before the national government became more complex, national supremacy asserted itself over states' rights. Over the nation's history, the national government has taken on new power and authority, often with the express consent of the states.

States and localities have acquired new functions as the power of the national government has increased. Obviously, they play a large role in implementing a wide array of federal programs. States and localities have in some ways become instruments of the federal government. They must distribute funds and enforce rules and regulations for programs that have been developed by Congress. This implementation function has also led to another, less obvious function for state and local governments. As beneficiaries of the federal grant system, they have become constituents for federal government programs. And, like other constituents, they have formed associations around their interests. Thus, the system of federalism has become a circular one, with the federal government formulating programs to be implemented by state and local governments, while the subnational governments lobby both Congress and the executive branch for favorable policies.

This arrangement has been in existence since the administration of President Franklin Roosevelt, who encouraged states and localities to join together in interest groups as a response to New Deal programs. The subnational governments have a particular interest in government social policy: they are the actors who must ultimately implement most social programs, they face the individual recipients of those programs on a daily basis, and they are considered, to some extent, "experts" in the provision of goods and services to their constituents. State and local governments play a unique role in the policymaking process. They are both recipients of federal largesse in the form of grants, and agents of the federal government in the fact that authority to run programs has been delegated to them. In addition to both of these roles, state and local governments are governmental entities in their own right, and must develop, debate and implement their own policies.

The most comprehensive study of state and local governments' lobbying effectiveness was published in 1974. In it, Donald Haider describes three phases in the government groups' history as lobbyists.[1] The first phase, which lasted from the New Deal through the early 1960s, was a period of direct federal-city relations. Local groups experienced increased prestige in Washington, and the emphasis on local programs set the stage for later competition between the state and local groups. Although the city groups were more prominent in the first phase, none of the groups was as actively involved in Washington as they would later become. The second phase of intergovernmental relations began in the mid-1960s. As the federal government increased its involvement in what had been state and local affairs, the groups began to compete with each other over which level of government would have control of the new programs. In this phase, the governors asserted themselves as critics of the new federal grant program. In some cases, the groups were able to unite in opposition to programs that they saw as undermining the authority of subnational governments.

The third phase began in 1969 with the Nixon presidency. According to Haider, this phase was marked by an increased prominence of the state and local groups. In addition, the Nixon administration made efforts to strengthen the state and local governments by directing both program authority and funding to the subnational governments. Nixon's "New Federalism" was intended to give the states and localities more control over federal grants. The high point of this period was the passage of general revenue sharing in 1972.

Haider studies eight cases of state and local lobbying in the second phase of intergovernmental lobbying, considering the government interest groups' activities, policy involvement and effectiveness, in addition to the external constraints faced by the groups.[2] He concludes that government lobbies have more legitimacy than other lobbies, by virtue of their political standing as subnational government actors, but that they act in a manner similar to that of private lobbying organizations.[3] The government groups have more access to the federal government than do other interest groups. In addition, they have had policy successes, particularly on issues that do not involve a substantial number of actors. However, "group lobbying activities where broad national policy questions are at stake still may be said to have a limited impact" (with the exception of revenue sharing, which was passed in the third phase of intergovernmental lobbying).[4]

The government groups' effectiveness in the 1960s and 1970s may have been a product of the times. Because the federal grant system was expanding during this phase, the political and economic environments were favorable to the groups' interest in receiving more federal money. In contrast, the current political environment is distinguished by decreasing federal grants and an increasing concern about the federal deficit. Indeed, cutbacks in federal spending have created a fourth phase of intergovernmental lobbying. While Haider's third phase was characterized by attempts to give the states more authority and more money, the fourth phase has been characterized by decreasing federal funding to the states.

The fourth phase began late in the Carter administration. Until then, federal grants to states and localities had been increasing, both in constant dollars and as a percentage of total state and local spending.[5] Table 1.1 illustrates the changes in federal grants-in-aid as a percentage of state and local expenditures throughout the four phases of intergovernmental lobbying. (Data is available only from 1955 on.) As is evident from Table 1.1, the fourth phase of intergovernmental lobbying marks a distinct change from the previous phases. The first three phases had in common that the grant system was expanding. In addition, from the New Deal through Nixon's New Federalism, there existed an underlying assumption that the federal government should be involved in state and local activities. The nature of that involvement was interpreted differently by various presidents. Roosevelt's New Deal established direct federal-city programs; Johnson's Great Society developed categorical grants to states, localities and non-governmental entities; Nixon's New Federalism consolidated grants and decentralized administration. None of these presidents challenged the idea that federal grants to the subnational governments were necessary and useful.

Federal grants to states and localities decreased during the period beginning in 1979. In addition, conceptions of federalism began to change in the fourth phase. Where the federal government had previously been the answer to state and local ailments, by the 1980s the federal government had become the problem. Reagan epitomized this new attitude. He attempted to decentralize government activity by decreasing federal funding. In his "turnback" proposal,

Table 1.1 Federal Grants-in-Aid

Year	Federal Grants as a Percentage of Total State and Local Expenditures	Percent Real Increase or Decrease from Total Federal Grant for Previous Year
Phase I:		
1955	10.2%	4.1%
1956	10.4	9.4
1957	10.5	6.5
1958	11.7	18.9
1959	14.1	30.7
1960	14.5	7.4
1961	13.7	0.4
1962	14.1	9.3
1963	14.2	5.9
1964	15.4	17.1
Phase II:		
1965	15.1	5.4
1966	16.1	14.7
1967	16.9	13.3
1968	18.3	16.1
Phase III:		
1969	17.8	2.6
1970	19.0	11.7
1971	19.7	9.2
1972	21.7	15.6
1973	24.0	15.2
1974	22.3	-4.8
1975	22.6	3.0
1976	24.1	10.4
1977	25.5	7.7
1978	26.5	5.9
Phase IV:		
1979	25.8	-2.7
1980	25.8	-0.7
1981	24.7	-4.9
1982	21.6	-12.4
1983	21.3	.7
1984	20.9	1.6
1985	20.9	4.3
1986	19.9	3.2
1987	18.0	-6.5
1988	17.7	2.1
1989	17.3	1.1
1990	17.9	7.7

Source: ACIR, *Significant Features of Fiscal Federalism 1991* (Washington: GPO, 1991), 2:50.

Reagan suggested that the federal government take over funding and administration of Medicaid, in exchange for giving states sole responsibility for Aid to Families with Dependent Children (AFDC) and some forty other programs.[6] However, the fourth phase did not begin with the Reagan administration. "Federal grants to states began decreasing in the latter half of the Carter administration. Federal grant outlays as a percentage of all federal spending had already declined 9% between fiscal 1978 and 1980, and federal aid as a percentage of Gross National Product (GNP) had declined 5%. Indeed, some advocates of greater federal social spending were aware by the early 1980s that a reversal of prior growth trends was inevitable."[7] Although Carter did not plan to change the system of federalism, he too ran on an anti-Washington platform, and his criticism of the Washington establishment helped pave the way for Reagan's "New Federalism."

Other factors contributed to the reversal of federal government growth. In the 1970s the combination of inflation and economic stagnation, the weakened presidency and decentralized Congress, the growing public dissatisfaction with and distrust of government all created a new environment that was less than favorable to a spiraling federal grant system.[8] In the 1980s the federal deficit added to the perception that the national government was out of control, and limited the development of new grant programs. From the late 1970s until 1990, the political and economic environments have were less favorable to increased federal spending.

This fourth phase of intergovernmental lobbying has put state and local governments in an interesting position. On the one hand, they are in a defensive posture, as they attempt to maintain federal spending on programs that would otherwise require increased state or local expenditures. On the other hand, they have an opportunity to decrease or eliminate federal regulations, thus regaining some power and authority. Throughout the fourth phase, state and local governments have faced cuts in the intergovernmental grant system. (Their biggest loss was the elimination of General Revenue Sharing [GRS]). More recently, however, they saw the passage of legislation restricting unfunded mandates, which by 1995 was as big a victory as had been the passage of GRS in 1972. Unfunded mandates are the exact opposite of what states and localities would like to see from the federal government. As money for new initiatives dwindled in the fourth phase, the federal government often imposed requirements on the subnational governments to implement policies at their own expense. Legislation restricting these requirements—which was originally introduced and defeated in 1990—moved the states and localities toward increased autonomy.

The importance of the state and local groups was institutionalized in the third phase, when increased competition for federal funds focused the groups' attention on Washington. However, a scarcity of federal funds made the groups more competitive, and may in fact have lessened their influence in social policy. For example, the state and local interest groups lost some of their clout in the executive branch during the Reagan administration. Since Reagan wanted state governments to take over some domestic policy functions, his administration was not favorably disposed to appeals from the subnational lobbying groups.[9] In addition, state and local groups themselves lost funding during the Reagan administration, leading to staff and operation reductions.[10]

> Ironically, it was state and especially local government organizations that were most dependent on federal subsidies and were most seriously affected by the Reagan cutbacks. These were the very organizations that the Nixon administration had consciously sponsored and assisted in order to provide lobbying assistance and technical support on behalf of common interests in the first New Federalism, but they were viewed as "wily stalkers of federal aid" or "merely [another] leg of that 'iron triangle'" by conservatives in the Reagan administration.[11]

Even as the subnational government groups were losing their clout as lobbyists for federal social spending, they were also becoming the focus of attention in a "new" system of federalism. Conservative calls for a devolution of social programs to the states gave them an increased prominence as innovators of public policy. However, such a devolution put the states in somewhat of a dilemma. Certainly, one of their primary goals has been to increase their authority over implementation and operation of programs. Conservative conceptions of a new federalism would give them that authority. But the states also want to get as much federal money as possible to help them to run social and other programs. Conservatives in the fourth phase have tried to decrease both federal spending and the "strings" attached to such spending. States would like the strings to be decreased or eliminated, but not the spending. And localities, on the front line for providing social services, are particularly concerned that the federal government continues to provide them the funds to do so.

Haider's research examines a time period during which the federal grant system was growing. States and localities want increased federal spending with as few federal strings attached as possible. The third phase of intergovernmental relations, characterized by revenue sharing and block grants, gave the state and local groups exactly what they wanted. In contrast, the fourth phase (from 1979 to at least 1990) created an unfavorable environment for the state and local groups. In light of the changes in federalism since 1974, there are compelling reasons for revisiting Haider's arguments. If the groups had success during a period of expanding federal grants, how well do they fare when the grant system is contracting? Do the tactics of the subnational interest groups differ in a period of declining federal spending? Are the groups perceived differently by federal actors than they were in the first three phases of intergovernmental relations? This book will examine three case studies from the late 1980s and early 1990 to answer those questions.

CASE SELECTION

This work examines three legislative acts passed during the fourth phase of intergovernmental lobbying: the Family Support Act of 1988, the Act for Better Child Care of 1990 and the Cranston-Gonzalez National Affordable Housing Act of 1990. Each of these acts represents an innovative social program, and each was characterized by state and local government lobbying. The acts were chosen from a universe of legislation upon which state and local associations claimed to have had an impact in the 100th and 101st Congresses. Such legislation was identified by information obtained from the following organizations: the National Governors' Association (NGA), the National Conference of State Legislatures (NCSL), the U.S. Conference of Mayors (USCM), the National Association of Counties (NACO) and the National League of Cities (NLC). Each organization provided information either through interviews (telephone or in-person) with association staff, or association publications concerning legislative priorities. Association staff were asked to identify legislation upon which they thought their organization had some impact and classify the legislation as "wins" or "losses." Similar information was acquired from association publications.

Table 1.2 summarizes the information provided by the organizations. If more than one association claimed to have had an impact on a particular act, that act is included in the table, with an indication as to whether the association claimed the act as a win or loss. A couple of caveats are in order here. First, a claim of success does not necessarily imply active lobbying on the part of the association. Congress may well have passed legislation in agreement with the association's legislative preferences without having been lobbied by that organization at all. No attempt was made at this point to have the interest groups characterize the extent of their lobbying efforts. Second, interest groups are generally reluctant to characterize any legislative activity as a loss. As is obvious from Table 1.2, most of the acts mentioned by the groups were "wins," not "losses." The staff of these organizations have few incentives to classify legislation as a loss since that would imply their own lobbying efforts were unsuccessful. Some groups claimed some legislation as both a win and a loss. It is probable that even legislation that was classified as a win may exclude provisions the association would have preferred or include provisions the association did not want. No attempt was made to verify the association's claims or clearly define success at this stage of the project.

Table 1.2 State and Local Government Groups' Positions on Legislation

	NGA	NCSL	NLC	USCM	NACO
Family Support Act (1988)	+	+/-	+	+	+/-
Anti-Drug Abuse Act (1990)		+		+	+/-
Child Care Act (1990)	+	+/-		+	+
McKinney Act Amendments (1990)	+		+	+	+
National Affordable Housing Act (1990)	+			+	+
Civil Rights Act (1990)		+	+	+	
JTPA Amendments (1988)	+		-	+	
JTPA Amendments (1990)			x	x	
Medicaid Expansions (1990)	-	-			
Head Start Amendments	+	+	+		
Farm Bill—Food Stamps (1990)					-
Catastrophic Health Care (1988)	-	-			+
Highway Obligation Ceiling Increase (1990)	+	+			+
Clean Air Act Reform (1990)	+	+/-		+	
Hazardous Materials Act	+	+	+		+
Reauthorization of Clean Water Act (1987)	+	+	+	+	
Farm Bill (1990)					+
Revenue Portion of Budget (1990)	-	-		+/-	+/-
Appropriations Portion of Budget (1990)		+			
Unfunded Mandate Legislation (1990)	x	x			

+ Legislation passed, group win   - Legislation passed, group loss
x Legislation did not pass, group loss   +/- Legislation passed, some provisions can be considered group win, others group loss

Table 1.2 represents the universe of legislation from which cases could be selected. The acts listed are those in which the groups had some interest, for which they may or may not have lobbied vigorously, and on which they may have had some impact. Table 1.3 divides the legislation into smaller groups by classifying it according to type of policy: distributive, redistributive, regulatory or other. Under this classification scheme, a policy is distributive if it provides governmental benefits for private actions that benefit society as a whole. Redistributive policies take wealth or benefits from one group or class and transfer them to another, less well-off group or class. Regulatory policies control private behavior in order to protect the public.[12] Cases have been selected from the redistributive acts, the most commonly mentioned legislation in Table 1.3. States and localities are more likely to lobby the federal government for redistributive than for other policies. According to Paul Peterson, this is because the subnational governments are unlikely to pursue policies that do not contribute to their own economic well-being. When the need for redistribution is pressing, the groups will lobby the federal government for such policies.[13] R. Allen Hays posits that both redistributive and regulatory policies will engender state and local lobbying at the federal level, since they both "impede economic growth if undertaken by a single unit in isolation."[14]

Hays also provides two reasons that may explain why redistributive policies were the focus of intergovernmental lobbying in the 1980s. The first he calls

Table 1.3 Types of Policies

Redistributive	Distributive
Family Support Act	Farm Bill
Anti-Drug Abuse Act	Highway Obligation Ceiling
McKinney Act Amendments	Increase
Civil Rights Act	
JTPA Amendments	Regulatory
Head Start Amendments	Clean Air Act
Medicaid Expansions	Hazardous Materials Act
Catastrophic Health Care	Reauthorization of Clean Water
Farm Bill—Food Stamps Provisions	Act
National Affordable Housing Act	
Child Care Provisions	Other
	Budget—revenue and
	appropriations
	Unfunded Mandate Legislation

the "threshold" explanation. States and localities are generally unwilling to become involved in redistributive activities. However, these governments will provide redistributive services to their constituents in response to need. When the subnational governments have assumed responsibility for such services, they are likely to turn to the federal government to assist in paying for them. "Once this role is established, these units will be under political pressure to maintain it, while at the same time minimizing their own expenditures. Therefore, they will see themselves as vitally affected by federal redistributive policies, and interest groups representing [the state and local governments] will be motivated to try to influence these policies."[15]

The second reason is what Hays calls the "risk" explanation. States and localities are likely to lobby for federal activity in an area when they believe there is a risk that they "will incur increased costs as a result of changes in that area."[16] During the 1980s, the state and local governments experienced increased demand for basic services such as housing, food and health care in response to cuts in federal spending for these services. Redistributive programs also formed the basis for Reagan's turnback proposal, in which the federal government would have assumed responsibility for Medicaid in return for state assumption of AFDC.[17] Thus, states and localities would find it logical to lobby for redistributive programs in response to both current need and future risk.

Within the redistributive category, legislation characterized by active lobbying was selected for study. Such legislation is similar to the cases selected by Haider. All of Haider's cases were of high importance to the state and local groups, both in terms of the amount of resources invested and the potential impact of the policies on group members.[18] Since the purpose of the research is to study the effectiveness of state and local group lobbying, it is important to study cases in which they lobbied extensively. Active lobbying indicates the importance of the case to the groups, and allows for a comparison of a wider variety of lobbying techniques.

Staff members of the appropriate committees or subcommittees in the House or Senate were asked to categorize the lobbying activity of the state and local groups on legislation. Table 1.4 classifies the legislation by level of lobbying activity. As would be predicted by Hays and Peterson, both redistributive and regulatory policies were the subject of "very active" intergovernmental lobbying. Of the six redistributive acts, three created new social programs (or, in the case of the Family Support Act, comprehensively reformed an existing social program); the others were amendments to or expansions of existing programs. The three major redistributive acts were selected because they represent a strong challenge for interest groups. One would expect lobbying organizations to have a greater impact on incremental than comprehensive change. Insofar as the groups were lobbying for broad policy initiatives, such lobbying would be less likely to be effective. In the legislative process, groups

Table 1.4 Level of State and Local Government Groups' Involvement

	Very Active Lobbying	Somewhat Active Lobbying	Not Very Active Lobbying
Redistributive	Family Support Act Medicaid Child Care Housing Farm Bill/Food Stamps JTPA Amendments	Head Start Amendments Anti-Drug Abuse Act McKinney Act Amendments	Civil Rights Act Clean Water Act
Regulatory	Clean Air Act Hazardous Materials Act Highway Obligation Ceiling Increase		

that concentrate on preserving the status quo have the advantage over groups that push for change.[19] In addition, given the fact that the fourth phase of intergovernmental lobbying involves decreased federal spending, one would not expect new federal grant programs to be passed. Jerome Murphy refers to such cases as "crucial sites." Crucial sites (or cases) are chosen because they are atypical and "contradict prevailing expectations."[20] Murphy notes that sites (cases) may also be selected for their differences (the diversity strategy). While the three redistributive cases mentioned are crucial, or atypical, a second reason for their selection is that there is some variation both among and within these acts. Among the legislative initiatives, the Family Support Act is said to be most significantly influenced by state and local lobbies. The National Governors Association is credited with putting welfare reform on the policy agenda, and was instrumental in the passage of the Family Support Act. At the other extreme, the state and local associations did not really take the lead in the Cranston-Gonzalez Act, but became involved after housing had been established as a priority within Congress. Within each act, each association may have been successful in adoption of some provisions, and unsuccessful in adoption of others. For example, the National Conference of State Legislatures (NCSL) considers the Act for Better Child Care to be in general agreement with NCSL policy, even though it includes a mandatory state child care voucher or certificate program, which NCSL opposed.[21]

Haider also selected his cases according to differences in the level of conflict among the interest groups. Although all of his cases involved active lobbying, there were varying amounts of conflict: minimal, intermediate and considerable. The three major redistributive cases with active lobbying from Table 1.4 mirror the typology set forth by Haider. Haider's minimal conflict cases were regulatory policies involving nonmaterial benefits. The passage of these minimal conflict bills would benefit each of the government groups and its members.[22] These cases were characterized by group cooperation. Welfare reform legislation (the Family Support Act) may fall into this category. Both state as well as local interest groups felt that they would benefit from any new welfare legislation. There was relatively little disagreement or conflict among the groups.

The cases in Haider's second, intermediate category were non zero-sum policies in which compromise among the groups was possible and acceptable to all the groups. Conflict in this category could be easily diffused.[23] Child Care legislation is consistent with this classification. While some conflict existed among the groups, there was no fear of moving benefits from one level of government to another. The third category of cases was essentially a zero-sum group. Passage of a policy would benefit one group at the expense of another. These cases pitted localities against states, and involved a good deal of conflict.[24] The National Affordable Housing Act falls into this category. There was disagreement between the state and local groups about the funding of new housing programs, and the groups perceived that increased benefits to one level of government would decrease benefits at the second level.

The three major redistributive cases are thus examples of crucial cases, which are similar in that they involve major lobbying efforts by some of the state and local groups. The cases are also different in that they represent differing levels of conflict among the groups. The similarities and differences of the cases reflect the similarities and differences of the cases selected for comparison by Haider.

A final reason for studying the three major redistributive acts is that they include two social welfare policies and one housing policy. Hays found that state and county groups were more likely to lobby for social welfare policies, because these governments have (albeit reluctantly) assumed responsibility for such policies, and want as much federal help as possible in funding for them. Cities have had relatively little involvement in redistributive policies, with the exception of low income housing.[25] Thus, the three cases provide an opportunity to study intensive lobbying efforts by all of the groups.

THE RESEARCH DESIGN

Data for this study has been gathered in four ways. First, interviews were conducted with congressional staff members—both majority and minority—from the committees and subcommittees in the House and Senate that had jurisdiction over the legislation. There were at least two committees with jurisdiction over each act. The Family Support Act was handled in the House by the Select Committee on Children, Youth and Families; the Ways and Means Committee (Subcommittee on Public Assistance); and the Agriculture Committee. In the Senate, the Finance Committee and Labor and Human Resources Committee (Subcommittee on Children and Family) had jurisdiction over the Family Support Act.

The Cranston-Gonzalez National Affordable Housing Act was examined by the House Banking, Finance and Urban Affairs Committee (Housing Subcommittee) and the Senate Banking, Housing and Urban Affairs Committee (Housing Subcommittee). The Act for Better Child Care fell under the jurisdiction of the House Select Committee on Children, Youth and Families; the House Education and Labor Committee (Subcommittee on Human Resources); the House Ways and Means Committee (Subcommittee on Human Resources); the Senate Labor and Human Resources Committee (Subcommittee on Children and Family and Subcommittee on Health); and the Senate Finance Committee.

Committee staff members who were involved in the passage of the legislation were interviewed. The interviews with these staff members were in-person and semi-structured, with the majority of the questions open-ended. The questions were designed to gather information on the role of the state and local associations in the passage of the legislation: what input each association had, whether the associations were acting in concert or separately, the methods by which each association acted (testifying, drafting legislation, etc.), whether the final legislation was in agreement with each association's initial desires and what other lobbying organizations had an interest in the legislation. In addition, opinion questions attempted to discern which actors had the most significant impact on the legislation, the importance of state and local interest groups in the passage of the legislation, how well the legislation met the preferences of the governmental lobbies, general attitudes of Congress members and staff toward state and local groups and the general influence of state and local groups in Congress. (Appendix 1 contains the interview guide for Congressional staff.)

Second, interviews were conducted with staff in the five associations. Again, these interviews were in-person and semi-structured, consisting primarily of open-ended questions. The information obtained includes (in addition to the information and opinions gathered from congressional staff) the legislative priorities of each association during the 100th and 101st Congresses. (Appendix 2 contains the interview guide for association staff.)

Third, information was gathered from the committee and subcommittee hearings and the floor debates and votes to analyze the testimony of state and local lobbies and its possible effects on the outcome of the relevant bills. In addition, association documents pertaining to their policies on the various issues were also examined to analyze the stated positions of the associations prior to passage of each of the acts.

Finally, articles on each of these bills in *Congressional Quarterly Weekly Reports*, the *New York Times*, the *Washington Post*, and other relevant publications, as well as committee and conference committee reports were used to develop a legislative history of each act and to determine the public perception of state and local associations' and other lobbies' roles in the passage of the legislation.

Various methods of information-gathering are needed in qualitative research. Interest groups are most appropriately studied through intensive methods designed to reveal complex processes. Interviews with congressional and association staff reveal perceptions of both actors regarding the role of interest groups in the process. By interviewing several different people from several committees and associations, perceptions, which are subjective, can be cross-checked and validated in a more objective manner. For example, if a staffperson from the U.S. Conference of Mayors says that her association had a large impact on the passage of the Family Support Act, it is solely her perception of the case, which may or may not be consistent with reality. However, if staff from the National Governors' Association and National Association of Counties as well as committee staff say that the USCM had a large impact, the perceptions reinforce one another and are more likely to be a true reflection of reality.

In addition, analysis of documents relating to each of the acts assists in validating the information obtained in interviews. If association staff claim that the child care provisions were consistent with their initial preferences, this can be verified by examining testimony and policy statements by the association in question. Document analysis may be somewhat more objective than interviews. This work uses several methods of obtaining and verifying information on several different cases. Such methods will assist in discovering complex decision-making processes and validating the perceptions of the individuals involved.

Interviews and Hypotheses

The bulk of the research involves the interviews with congressional and interest group staff. Although most of the interview questions were open-ended, several closed-ended questions about lobbying group influence were also asked. Both the lobbyists and the congressional staff were asked to rate (on a scale of one to ten) the overall influence of interest groups as well as their influence on the particular legislation and the attitudes of congressional staff and members toward the state and local interest groups. The data are thus based on perceptions of influence. Such perceptions are obviously subjective, but may also provide an overall picture of group influence. Since both policymakers and those attempting to influence policy were asked the same questions, the subjectivity will be moderated.[26]

The interview guide was designed to test several hypotheses about the role of state and local groups in the policymaking process.

1. State and local governments are more likely to be effective when they act in concert with each other.

2. State and local interest groups are more likely to be effective when they act in a coalition with other interest groups.

3. State associations are more likely to be effective than local associations in the Senate; local associations are more likely to be effective than state associations in the House.

4. Tactics used by state and local governments are similar to tactics used by other interest groups.

5. State and local interest groups have more access to congressional members and staff than other interest groups.

6. State and local interest groups are more likely to be effective in concrete, specific provisions than on abstract policy issues.

Effectiveness was determined by comparing each association's stated goals with provisions of the three acts, by documenting congressional staff's perceptions of each association's effectiveness, and by analyzing pertinent documents, as noted previously.

The first two hypotheses refer to alliances, either among the government groups themselves or more broadly, with other interest groups. When the federal grant system was expanding, states and localities did not often act together; they were competing for control of funding and administration of programs. Since federal spending is decreasing, one would predict that states and localities would act together, because some funding is better than none, regardless of how it is distributed.

Open-ended questions in the interview guide dealt specifically with alliances and their effects on the process. Alliances are formed in order to increase the number of individuals represented by the groups. Generally, alliances strengthen group legitimacy. It is possible that coalitions with other groups dilute the legitimacy of state and local groups. If they are perceived by Congress as having more legitimacy than other groups, then subnational lobbyists could better exploit that legitimacy by acting alone or in coalitions with other governmental groups.

The concept of legitimacy refers to the perceived status of a particular group. According to Haider, the state and local groups have greater legitimacy (or higher status) than other groups, which gives them increased access to Congress and the executive branch. Haider distinguishes between the broad interests of the state and local groups and the narrow interests of other groups. State and local governments are public actors. The state and local government interest groups are made up of elected officials who represent the interests of their constituents in contrast to private lobbying groups whose interests are confined to a more narrow area. Actors in Congress and the executive branch often accord the state and local government groups more legitimacy because of their status as elected officials.[27] However, the state and local groups' interests may be just as narrow as those of other interest groups. Although they are involved in a broad range of policies, the government groups' overriding concern is in maintaining their spatial interests. The status that these groups have comes not from their interests, as Haider implies, but from their membership. Since the government groups are made up of elected officials, they have a great deal in common with members of Congress. Representatives often started out as state legislators or city or county officials, and Senators may have been (or may contemplate becoming) state governors. There exists a level of understanding between members of Congress and the government groups that is not present with other interest groups. The government groups are lobbyists who themselves have been lobbied, and this gives them a special status among members of Congress.

In addition, state and local governments are the level at which many federal policies are implemented. This also increases their status. For example, in welfare reform, Representatives and Senators wanted to get input from the governors, many of whom had been implementing their own innovative work-welfare programs. Hypothesis 3 posits that the level of government of the interest group (state or local) will have an impact on the level of access in the two chambers of Congress (House and Senate). In addition, the perceived legitimacy of the state and local groups may affect their tactics, access and effectiveness, addressed in the remaining hypotheses.

Hypothesis 4 deals with the tactics of interest groups. Tactics are a means to an end: influencing policy. There are two reasons why state and local interest groups may use different tactics than other groups: first, they have less money than private interest groups, so they would be more likely to use the less costly methods, for example, mobilizing grassroots, acting in coalitions. Second, their legitimacy as governmental actors may make them more likely to use tactics that exploit that status. Their status as elected officials who understand the needs of other elected officials and who implement federal policies may be exploited through meetings with congressional members and staffs, as well as testimony at hearings. In addition, the combination of tactics that the state and local groups use may be different from the combination used by other groups. Berry defines an outside strategy as one that involves media and grassroots mobilization and an inside strategy as one that involves testimony, meetings and campaign contributions. Haider found that state and local groups use a combination of inside and outside tactics including personal contact with congressional staff and grassroots mobilization. This is probably because, like private groups, they are insiders, but like public groups, they recognize the power of mobilizing their constituents.

Whether or not the tactics of the state and local interest groups are similar to other interest groups may help to clarify their status. If they use similar tactics to public groups, then maybe it is appropriate to place them in this category. If their tactics are a hybrid of those of public and private interest groups, then perhaps state and local groups are in a separate category. Their status as governmental actors may make certain tactics more useful for them than for other groups. Thus the tactics they use may be an indication of the access and legitimacy of these groups.

Several open-ended interview questions relate to the tactics of the interest groups. Some are general; some ask about specific tactics (drafting legislation, personal contact with congressional staff, use of media).

Hypothesis 5, that state and local interest groups have more access than other interest groups, refers to the ability of government groups to be heard in Congress. The legitimacy of these groups may mean that they have more access than other interest groups, that they find it easier to meet with Representatives and Senators and their staffs, and that their opinions are important in policy decisions. Open and closed-ended questions in the interview guide ask what kind of reception both association members and staff groups receive in Congress, how willing congressional staff are to meet with or talk to association staff and whether the attitudes of members and their staffs are favorable or unfavorable toward the state and local interest groups.

State and local groups had a great deal of access in the 1960s and 1970s, when the federal government was substantially involved in state and local policies. As the federal government distances itself from state and local policies, then the access of the groups may decrease. If it does not, then the groups' access comes from their status (legitimacy) as elected officials, not from the prevailing notions of federalism.

The final hypothesis is that state and local groups are more effective on concrete legislative provisions than on more abstract policy goals. Other groups may set the agenda and formulate the policies for debate, while the government groups play a more important role in making compromises on specific provisions of policies that have been proposed already. Such compromises make legitimation possible. This hypothesis is useful for illustrating differences among the three acts, by determining the extent of the associations' impact on particular provisions and the overall outcome. The interview guide includes questions about the effectiveness of the interest groups on specific provisions of the legislation, on the overall passage of legislation, and about the groups' role in developing policy.

The overarching question of the research is how effective the state and local groups are as lobbying organizations. Their effectiveness will be determined by the responses of the groups and congressional staff to questions on influence. The groups' tactics will be related to their influence. Were certain tactics more likely to be used for legislation characterized as being influenced by the groups? Were the groups more likely to act in a coalition for such legislation? Or was the groups' influence muted by coalitions?

The perceptions of group influence will also be compared to the groups' initial goals for the legislation. What did the groups actually get out of the legislation? Does the legislation represent a significant change from previous policy and is it generally congruent with group preferences at the beginning of the legislative process?

Finally, group effectiveness will be related to the policy and political environments. Has competition among groups increased? Is it more or less difficult to influence federal social policy in the fourth phase of intergovernmental lobbying? Have state and local government groups' effectiveness and access increased or decreased relative to Haider's findings?

The following chapter places the study of state and local interest groups in the context of the interest group literature. Chapters 3, 4 and 5 are case studies of the government groups' role in legislation. Chapter 3 deals with child care provisions, which were significantly influenced by state and local groups. Child care legislation involved a moderate level of conflict among the groups, which used their access effectively to act as facilitators for the legislation. Chapter 4 examines the National Affordable Housing Act, which had the highest level of conflict among the groups, and consequently the lowest level of influence. Chapter 5 is a study of the Family Support Act, which was characterized by minimal conflict among the groups and a high level of lobbying by the National Governors Association. The NGA had a high level of access and a large impact on the final legislation. Chapter 6 places the case studies in the context of the fourth phase of intergovernmental lobbying, drawing comparisons to Haider and reexamining the hypotheses. The research should place state and local interest groups in a new context. First, it will attempt to define more clearly their classification, based on their membership and lobbying techniques. Second, it will reexamine the access of the state and local groups. Finally, it will provide an analysis of the groups' activities in a different policy environment and thus furnish a basis for comparison to Haider's findings.

NOTES

1. Donald Haider, *When Governments Come to Washington: Governors, Mayors and Intergovernmental Lobbying* (New York: The Free Press, 1974), pp. 48–75.

2. Ibid., p. 212.

3. Ibid., p. 256.

4. Ibid., p. 288.

5. Advisory Commission on Intergovernmental Relations, *Significant Features of Fiscal Federalism*, 2 vols. (Washington: U.S. Government Printing Office, October 1991), 2:50.

6. Larry Sabato, *Goodbye to Good-time Charlie* (Washington: Congressional Quarterly Press, 1983), p. 168.

7. Timothy Conlan, *New Federalism: Intergovernmental Reform from Nixon to Reagan* (Washington: The Brookings Institution, 1988), pp. 156–157.

8. Ibid., pp. 100–106.

9. See B. J. Reed, "The Changing Role of Local Advocacy in National Politics," *Journal of Urban Affairs* 5 (1983): 287–298; and Charles H. Levine and James A. Thurber, "Reagan and the Intergovernmental Lobby: Iron Triangles, Cozy Subsystems and Political Conflict," in *Interest Group Politics,* 2nd ed., ed. Allan Cigler and Burdett A. Loomis (Washington: Congressional Quarterly Press, 1986), pp. 202–220.

10. Conlan, p. 178.

11. Ibid., pp. 158–159.

12. See Theodore Lowi, "American Business, Public Policy, Case Studies and Political Theory," *World Politics* 16 (July 1964): 677–715; Randall Ripley and Grace A. Franklin, *Congress, the Bureaucracy and Public Policy* (Homewood, Ill.: The Dorsey Press, 1984); and R. Allen Hays, "Intergovernmental Lobbying: Toward an Understanding of Priorities," *Western Political Quarterly* 44 (December 1991): 1081–1098. Hays distinguishes between "predominantly redistributive" and "partially redistributive" and adds a category, "developmental," which includes policies that contribute to local growth. This category was excluded here because none of the policies mentioned fell into it.

13. Paul Peterson, *City Limits* (Chicago: University of Chicago Press, 1981).

14. Hays, "Intergovernmental Lobbying," p. 1084.

15. Ibid., p. 1094.

16. Ibid., p. 1095.

17. Aid to Families with Dependent Children, which was substantially modified by the Family Support Act.

18. Haider, *When Governments Come to Washington*, p. 112.

19. Carol S. Greenwald, *Group Power, Lobbying and Public Policy* (New York: Praeger Publishers, 1977), pp. 197–198.

20. Jerome T. Murphy, *Getting the Facts: A Fieldwork Guide for Evaluators and Policy Analysts* (Santa Monica: Goodyear Publishing Co., Inc., 1980), p. 41.

21. National Conference of State Legislatures, *State-Federal Issue Brief: Summary of the 101st Congress, Second Session* (Denver: NCSL, 1990), pp. 5 and 9.

22. Haider, *When Governments Come to Washington*, p. 112.

23. Ibid.

24. Ibid.

25. Hays, "Intergovernmental Lobbying," pp. 1094–1095.

26. See William Gormley, *The Politics of Public Utility Regulation* (Pittsburgh: University of Pittsburgh Press, 1983), chapter 5.

27. Haider, *When Governments Come to Washington*, p. 229.

Chapter 2

State and Local Governments as Interest Groups

Interest groups are an integral part of the American political process. Their proliferation was encouraged by the founders as a method of ensuring minority rights in a system based on majority rule.[1] Subnational governments (states, cities and counties) formed their own interest groups starting in the 1930s. Since then, these groups have lobbied the federal government on behalf of states and localities. The shifting relationship among the federal, state and local governments may affect the success of subnational governments as interest groups. The government groups would like to increase federal money and decrease federal regulations. Whether they get their wishes depends on the prevailing political environment and current conceptions of federalism.

State and local government associations form a unique type of interest group. First, state and local associations mirror the constituency of Congress. State organizations of governors and legislatures represent the same constituents as senators; local organizations of mayors, cities and counties in some cases overlap with the constituents of representatives. Second, we most often think of interest groups as associations of private individuals that appeal to the government for their own private interest or for their perception of the public interest. In contrast, state and local interest groups are associations of public officials. They appeal to the national government for the interests of the subnational governments. They are lobbyists who themselves have been lobbied. Finally, the state and local groups are more concerned with the administration and funding of policies than with the substance of policies. These groups have an interest in maintaining or increasing their authority over federally funded programs.

This work examines state and local government lobbying in a new political and economic environment. Three case studies will be used to illustrate the lobbying tactics and legislative success or failure of the groups in the fourth phase of intergovernmental lobbying. The three cases, the Family Support Act (1988), the Act for Better Child Care (1990), and the Cranston-Gonzalez National Affordable Housing Act (1990) have common features. Each of these established a new social program, each created new federal funding, and each was characterized by active lobbying on the part of state and local government associations. A study of these three acts will illuminate the interest group role of state and local governments in a time period of decreasing federal grants.

The tactics of the five state and local lobbying groups (the National League of Cities, the U.S. Conference of Mayors, the National Association of Counties, the National Conference of State Legislatures and the National Governors' Association)[2] will be examined, as well as the constraints faced by each group. The groups will be treated as interest groups, thus, the remainder of this chapter examines the state and local lobbies in the context of interest group literature.

ACCESS

Traditional interest group theory, in the 1950s and 1960s, focused on how interest groups fit into democratic theory. The pluralist school of thought, as exemplified by David Truman in 1951,[3] posited that interest groups aid a democracy by allowing competing interests access to government decision-makers, who, in response to competition among groups, create compromises that are roughly equivalent to public preferences. Opponents of this theory, most notably Theodore Lowi, countered that pluralism is only a rationalization for a government that is unduly influenced by interest groups, a government that is not accountable to the public and that is incapable of acting in the broad public interest.[4]

In 1960, E. E. Schattschneider advocated strengthened political parties as a remedy for interest group dominance.[5] Since then, the political party system has continued to decline in the United States, and the importance of interest groups has increased. Interest groups now provide several functions that were once filled by the parties, including linking their constituents to the government, affording them the opportunity to participate, educating the American public, and setting the public policy agenda.[6] Decentralized political parties have provided increased opportunities for interest group participation.[7]

In order to participate in the governmental process, interest groups must have access to decision-makers. The problem is that all groups do not have equal access; some are more likely to be heard than others. In a system that is biased toward those groups that have access, the question is how to gain it. The three determinants of a group's effective access are its strategic position in society, its internal characteristics, and the institution that it is lobbying.[8] These three factors allow state and local interest groups a unique advantage. Access to Congress, the White House and executive agencies is easier for state and local groups because they have prestige, national membership and national orientation.[9]

The governmental lobbies' advantage in gaining access is due to their "public official status." The state and local lobbies are, for the most part, groups of elected officials. In a democracy, elected official status accords increased access, even across levels of government. "These groups constitute a kind of 'third house' of elected representatives at the national level."[10] Increased access may or may not lead to increased influence. Access "is simply a route towards influence, and in many cases, the route is blocked."[11]

Because access is an important precondition for influence, it raises questions about the representativeness of our government. If governmental lobbies have more access to federal institutions than other groups, does this contribute to or detract from the pluralistic tendencies of American government? On the one hand, governmental groups have more access because they are representative by their very nature. On the other hand, state and local lobbies represent the subnational governments themselves in addition to (and sometimes instead of) their citizens. Thus, their very existence may be at odds with democratic theory.[12]

Although Haider found that the state and local groups had an advantage over other groups in access to federal government institutions, this advantage may be diminished in the current political environment. As the federal grant system has declined, the government groups have lost some of their clout, particularly in the executive branch. Access to federal institutions increased during the first three phases of intergovernmental relations, when the groups were the beneficiaries of new federal policies. One of the questions of this research is whether and how access changed in the fourth phase of lobbying. As the groups lost favor in the fourth phase, did they also find it more difficult to make their voices heard in Congress? Or did congressional actors turn to the state and local groups for assistance in making difficult choices about the distribution of limited funds?

CLASSIFICATION

Access is important for interest groups because their most important function is lobbying. Without access, there can be no influence, and thus no reason to lobby. Lester Milbrath defined lobbying as attempting to influence governmental decision-making through direct or indirect communication.[13] Governmental organizations, like other interest groups, lobby the federal government to achieve their policy ends. In fact, "some of the most powerful attempts to influence decisions are directed by government officials against other government officials."[14] Although all interest groups are alike in that they attempt to influence government, they differ in the policies for which they lobby and in their members, who are the expected beneficiaries of those policies. Classifications of interest groups have been made based on policy interests and on membership.

A useful distinction based on policy areas is that between private interest groups and public interest groups. A public interest group differs from a private one in that it "seeks a collective good which will not materially benefit only the members or activists."[15] State and local interest groups have traditionally been placed in this category, along with the many liberal groups that were formed in the 1970s around particular policy areas such as the environment, the women's movement and the anti-war movement, among others. It also later applied to conservative groups that were formed in the 1980s around traditional morals and family values.

State and local groups have continued to be classified as public interest groups, almost by default. They do not represent private interests, and they consist of public officials, so it has been assumed that they are public interest groups. Insofar as these groups "seek a collective good" then they should be classified as public interest groups. Whether this is the proper classification rests on whether their interests materially benefit a broader group than the members or activists. When big city governments lobby for programs that benefit urban areas at the expense of rural areas, is this a broad public good? When state governments seek federal funding for state programs, who is materially benefited? State and local groups fit into the category of public interest groups mainly because they are made up of public officials. However, they do not have the same conception of "collective good" that other public interest groups have. According to Haider, the groups' public official composition accords them public interest status. The government groups capitalize on this status, which assists them in their lobbying activities. As public interest groups, they are tax exempt, and they are set apart from other, private interest groups. [16]

In fact, state and local interest groups differ from other public interest groups in that they are lobbying for the interests of their respective governments, not those of the governments' constituents. The interests of the governmental lobbies involve the allocation of resources, and may or may not coincide with the interests of the citizens of those governments.[17] In the 1960s and 1970s, when government interest groups increased their lobbying role, their efforts were focused on greater state and/or local control over federal grant programs. For example, the U.S. Conference of Mayors had some difficulty with the implementation of the Economic Opportunity Act of 1964, chiefly because private organizations (Community Action Agencies) were allowed to take on governmental authority. Although one of the purposes of the act was to give private citizens more decision-making authority, the mayors eventually were successful in regaining this authority from the Community Action Agencies.[18] In such a situation, the mayors lobbied for themselves as governments, not for their constituents, who may have preferred greater citizen involvement in the program.

Haider describes a difference between a spatial or geographic interest, and a functional or policy interest.[19] Government lobbies have a spatial interest (maintaining authority over their own geographic sphere) as well as a functional (policy) interest. While government lobbies are interested in particular policies, they, unlike other groups (or at least to a greater extent than other groups), are also interested in the spatial dimension of any policy, that is, who will have the authority in implementation and control over the funds. While other public interest groups are generally formed around one particular policy area (housing, child care, environment, welfare rights), governmental interest groups form around a functional area (state or local government) that encompasses several policy areas. In one way, state and local interests are broader than those of other public interest groups: they are interested in a wide variety of domestic policies that are implemented at the state and local level. In another way, their policy interests are narrower. Subnational governments are interested in the process of policy (that is, who implements it) to a greater extent than its outcomes.

Another way to classify interest groups is by the types of individuals, rather than the policies, they represent. Jack Walker divides interest groups into two main groups: occupational and non-occupational. Non-occupational interest groups are those that have open membership; occupational interest groups form around the profession of their members and consist of the profit sector, the non-profit sector and mixed sectors.[20] Again, state and local interest groups do not fit neatly into the classification scheme, although there is a better fit than in the distinction between public and private groups. Government groups can be classified as occupational, because membership is based on profession (members of the National Governors' Association, for example, are governors). They are non-profit, but they are different from other non-profits in that they represent governmental organizations.

It appears that governmental lobbies are indeed a "special breed of interest group."[21] Perhaps they should be in their own separate category. That is, if we classify groups according to policies, there would be three types: public groups (which represent public interest policies), private groups (which represent special interests) and government groups (which represent the interests of the state and local governments). Or, if we classify according to membership, occupational interest groups should consist of four types: profit sector, non-profit sector, mixed sector and government sector.

Finally, although it is difficult to place governmental interest groups in a broader classification scheme, it is easier to make classifications within the category of government groups. There are two main types of government interest groups. The first type consists of the five general government groups: the National Association of Counties, the National League of Cities, the U.S.

Conference of Mayors, the National Conference of State Legislatures and the National Governors' Association. These groups are generalists, and are the "public interest" governmental groups. The second category are the public official organizations, associations concerned with specific government programs.[22] These include such groups as the American Public Welfare Association (APWA) and the National Association of Housing Redevelopment Officials (NAHRO), groups that were involved in the passage of welfare reform and the housing bill, respectively. Studies of state and local groups have concentrated on the first category, the generalists. This work will be no exception, although public official organizations will be discussed where they had a significant role in legislation.

In the fourth phase of intergovernmental lobbying, the distinction between the government groups and other public interest groups becomes more important. Throughout the 1960s and 1970s, the federal grant system was a centralizing force which increased national involvement in state activities by increasing both federal funding and regulation of domestic programs. Cuts in federal spending represent a decentralizing trend. Reagan's New Federalism was a further decentralizing force, since he attempted to move the federal government out of some activities he felt were more appropriate for states.[23] This decentralization exacerbates the differences between the spatial interests of the government groups and the functional interests of other public interest groups. State and local groups attempt to maintain or augment their relative share of dwindling federal resources, fighting for authority over programs where possible. The groups become more protective of their spatial interests when they find themselves losing funding or authority. Other groups are interested in ensuring that their policy concerns are addressed, regardless of how the programs are administered or the funds are distributed.

FORMATION

The three major theories about the formation of interest groups are the "disturbance" theory set forth by David Truman, the "exchange" or "entrepreneur" theory of Robert Salisbury and Mancur Olson's selective benefits theory. Truman's disturbance theory stated that interest groups are formed in complex societies when an event occurs that changes the equilibrium and brings individuals together.[24] Salisbury's theory argues that it is not an event but an entrepreneur that causes individuals to form groups. The entrepreneur offers an exchange to persons for joining the group: group benefits are traded for group membership.[25] Salisbury's theory expanded on previous literature that had proposed three incentives for group membership: joining a group may benefit an individual materially (material benefits), give him or her the opportunity to interact with like-minded individuals (solidary benefits) or allow the individual to pursue a particular aim (purposive benefits).[26] Mancur Olson added that, to avoid the "free rider" effect, interest group benefits must be selective, that is, they must accrue only to members of the group.[27]

The state and local groups have evolved over time, and it is difficult to classify their formation. Both the governors and the mayors formed groups because of presidential involvement. The National Governors' Association (originally, the Governors Conference) began in 1908, when President Theodore Roosevelt invited thirty-four governors to the White House to support his natural resource legislation. The U.S. Conference of Mayors was formed with President Franklin D. Roosevelt's active involvement, and was intended to increase the role of the cities in new national programs. If the President can be considered an interest group entrepreneur, then the groups were established in response to entrepreneurship. The President convinced the governmental actors that it was to their advantage to form an interest group. They would achieve both material benefits (increased federal funding) and purposive benefits (achieving policy goals on substantive issues).

State and local interest groups became active participants in the federal arena when the relationship between the federal government and its subnational governments began to change. The Great Depression was the initial impetus for the state and particularly local governments to begin lobbying the federal government. With the rise in federal grants-in-aid and the increase of federal-local programs starting with the Great Society, state and local groups became active lobbyists, attempting to influence the federal government to increase its allocation of resources to subnational governments, and sometimes battling with each other over administrative authority. From this perspective, it appears that the governmental groups became entrenched as lobbying groups due to a "disturbance," the Great Society, which changed the nature of the federal grant system. Also, since the grant system sometimes favored one level of government over another, the subnational governments found themselves in a position where they could lobby for selective benefits. What profited the local groups did not necessarily profit the state groups, and vice versa. The nature of the federal grant system changed again in the 1980s. Cuts in grants to states created another "disturbance" that may have changed the lobbying efforts of the state and local groups.

TECHNIQUES

Interest groups of any kind are, by their very nature, seeking to influence governmental actions. Influence is attempted by communicating information to governmental institutions. In fact, lobbying consists of "the stimulation and transmission of a communication by someone other than a citizen acting on his own behalf, directed to a governmental decisionmaker with the hope of influencing his decision."[28] Interest groups use various tactics to communicate information in an attempt to influence governmental actors. Jeffrey Berry classifies three types of interest group tactics: direct (presentations, testifying, formal legal action), through constituents (exhorting them to write letters, attend protest demonstrations) and indirect (donating money through political action committees [PACs], publishing voting records and research results and organizing public relations campaigns).[29]

Lobbying groups have long-range plans (or policies), strategies to fulfill those plans, and tactics (or specific actions) to implement those strategies.[30] Specific tactics are chosen based on the group strategy for a particular issue. One study differentiates between "inside" and "outside" strategies. An outside strategy, which involves the use of free or paid media (indirect tactic) and may also include mobilizing grassroots support (constituent tactic), is used when there is a large amount of conflict and group opposition to a bill. An inside strategy, which involves testimony, meetings with congressional members and staff (direct), and campaign contributions (indirect), is most useful when there is little conflict on a bill.[31]

Governmental interest groups are more likely to use inside tactics or a combination of inside and outside tactics in lobbying at the national level. State and local interest groups rely on personal contact with both the executive and legislative branches, mobilization of their publics and the use of paid professional staff.[32] Although inside tactics are generally used by other interest groups when there is little conflict on a bill, they are used by government groups even when conflict exists. This is because state and local groups are insiders themselves, and inside tactics best exploit their status. The governors and mayors are particularly interested in exploiting their status as chief executives. The subnational chief executives often find that the least expensive and most politically expedient strategy is to work with fellow executives. Personal contact enables them to capitalize on their strongest asset.[33]

Because their memberships are so diverse, and because there is often conflict both within and among the groups, state and local lobbyists tend to use low-profile tactics. For example, when lobbying for revenue sharing, the states and localities were divided as to which level of government should receive and distribute the funds. The government groups used staff negotiations with Wilbur Mills (then chair of the House Ways and Means Committee), pressure from Democratic state and local group members on congressional Democrats, direct appeals to other Ways and Means Committee members, lobbying of all Representatives and grassroots support.[34]

During the Johnson administration, the mayors concentrated their lobbying efforts on the President, because they implemented the new presidential programs and because the Democratic President's electoral strategy depended upon the support of the big cities.[35] Mayors distributed research findings, mobilized grassroots and used telephone, mail and personal contact, but they did not use the media, public relations campaigns, endorsement of candidates (despite the presidential reliance on big city electoral support), contribution of money or publishing voting records.[36] Mayors use similar tactics today; however, their relationship with the President has eroded over time. The mayors have remained Democratic; the office of the presidency was for twelve years filled by Republicans. In addition, Reagan's attempts to cut back the federal government's role in domestic policy meant that the mayors no longer had the same clout as when Johnson was expanding direct federal city programs.

The lobbying behavior of the state and local government groups is very similar to the behavior of other interest groups.[37] The most visible technique of any interest group is testifying at congressional hearings. This method, like bumper stickers for political campaigns, is generally more noteworthy for its absence than it is effective for its presence. It is the most obvious method of communicating information, if not the most effective. Testimony "is often seen as a defensive action that dare not be neglected."[38] State and local government groups use this technique as much as any other group. They take advantage of their national memberships which overlap with congressional constituencies and provide witnesses from committee members' states or districts.[39] In child care, welfare and housing, all of the interest groups testified before congressional committees, although in some instances this was the extent of a group's lobbying efforts.

MEMBERSHIP AND GROUP RESOURCES

Governmental interest groups are unique in that their membership consists of elected officials. This affects their relationship to the national government, as we have seen, by affording access to the groups. It also affects their lobbying tactics and resources. The membership of the groups is, in some ways, their greatest strength as well as their greatest weakness. Particularly for the city lobbies, membership is diverse. The USCM represents big cities, while the NLC represents smaller cities, but even within each organization there are cleavages that reflect those in the nation as a whole: regional differences, party and ideological differences, differences in city size.[40] The National Association of Counties also has open cleavages. Because there are tensions between the different factions, the groups tend to avoid controversial issues and develop policy through committees.[41]

The governors have their own problems with members. The NGA is an association of "fifty prima donnas" who are each politically prominent. As a matter of fact, it may be more difficult for the NGA to achieve consensus than for the USCM, which has a much larger constituency. Governors are more likely to take a forceful stand and, due to their national prominence, make their voices heard. Mayors are individually less well-known and less conspicuous, and disproportionately Democratic.[42] This is not to say that the mayors are monolithic. Although the USCM's membership is less diverse and unwieldy than the NLC's, it is still difficult for the mayors to agree. They, as well as other government officials, tend to act for their own rather than group interests. The biggest problem with the USCM has always been its "lack of internal cohesion." For this reason, the group is more useful in lobbying for general legislation.[43]

Other resources besides membership may affect an interest group's lobbying. These include the group's geographical distribution, its organizational and leadership resources, and its place in the economic and social environment.[44] State and local interest groups have advantages in all of these areas. Their geographical distribution is national. All of the groups have professional lobbying staff located in Washington, which gives them strong organizational and leadership resources. The NGA's leadership resources are enhanced by the national prominence of its members, who receive a great deal of attention when they speak out in favor of a governmental policy, as was evident in welfare reform. Because the groups represent entities that receive government funding and implement government programs, they have an important place in the economic and social environment. Economically, they are not as strong as some groups because they do not make monetary political contributions.

Overall, the state and local government interest groups have strong resources, the most important of which is their public official status, which translates into increased access. Their weakest characteristic is their lack of internal cohesion.

COALITIONS AND POLICY SUBSYSTEMS

One characteristic of interest groups is that they do not act alone. Interest groups may join together with other groups in temporary or more permanent alliances. A temporary alliance is known as a coalition, and is usually built around a specific bill. A more permanent alliance is known as an issue network or policy subsystem. State and local groups act in concert with each other and with other groups, usually in a temporary coalition. There is some evidence to support the idea that the Conference of Mayors is also part of an urban policy subsystem. Alliances, whether they are temporary or permanent, have three overall effects on the democratic process:

1. They promote stability by making compromises outside of government institutions.

2. They allow groups to disseminate information and diffuse opposition.

3. They broaden the groups' focus of attention.[45]

Coalitions of interest groups are inevitable in a pluralistic, democratic society. Interest groups themselves are influential because they represent a large number of people; when they join together, they increase their representativeness. Alliances strengthen groups' demands in a system based on majority rule. As groups lobby for particular legislation, they note which other groups have similar views and, where possible, attempt to present a unified case to governmental decision-makers (particularly members of Congress). "Coalitions are 'action sets,' temporary alliances for limited purposes."[46]

State and local interest groups have in common that they wish the federal government to increase their monetary resources. The expansion of the federal grant system in the second phase of intergovernmental lobbying, however, created a division between the state and local groups. War on Poverty programs were essentially federal-city programs, with funds going directly to localities, rather than being channeled through the states. In many cases, state and local governments were in opposition to one another over the proper funding formula for government programs. Such opposition sometimes, but not always, created coalitions split along state-local lines. For example, the Omnibus Crime Control and Safe Streets Act of 1968, which created a direct federal-local law enforcement program, was supported by the USCM, the NLC and NACO. The National Governors' Conference, as it was then called, opposed the bill because it bypassed the states, and organized a coalition of state attorneys general and state law enforcement officials to request more state control.[47] In the current period, a scarcity of federal funds may make the government groups more competitive. In lobbying for the National Affordable Housing Act, the state and local groups were divided over what proportion of the funds should go to each level of government.

On the other hand, the need for a new policy and/or increased funds can encourage group alliances even when there is disagreement over the allocation of funds. Such was the case with revenue sharing in the third phase of intergovernmental relations. State and local governments, although they disagreed as to how the funds should be distributed, formed a coalition supporting revenue sharing legislation in 1967, and were able to develop a compromise on funding. Revenue sharing thus marks the high point in the coalition efforts of the governmental groups.[48] More recently, state and local groups have joined coalitions supporting child care legislation. Although there was disagreement over which governmental entity should have fiscal and administrative authority over such programs, the government groups were able to unite in their overall desire for national child care legislation.

State and local groups also form coalitions with other interest groups. In many cases, local groups have an interest in legislation that is of tangential concern to state groups. The local government groups form coalitions with like-minded interest groups, while state groups stay out of the issue altogether, or pursue only limited lobbying techniques. In the 1960s and 1970s, this was largely the case with housing programs. The mayors joined together with large coalitions on urban policy, and were successful in housing legislation because they were part of the coalitions that pushed for omnibus programs encompassing housing.[49] In fact, the mayors' alliance with other groups in this area revealed a more permanent alliance that also involved federal government actors, an alliance that has been called an "urban policy subsystem."[50]

The concept of a policy subsystem is an alternative to the more rigid iron triangle. Iron triangles describe fixed, closed systems consisting of the subcommittee, the bureaucracy and the interest groups in a particular policy area, such as defense. In theory, iron triangles have control over their policy area to such an extent that other actors cannot break in. Hugh Heclo challenged the idea of iron triangles, saying instead that there are more fluid "issue networks" which flow in and out of several policy areas.[51] The idea of an iron triangle has become an outdated notion, particularly since Congress itself has changed in such a way that more groups are afforded more access. Congressional fragmentation, budget deficits and enhanced representation of interests has led to a "new policy environment," one that involves more openness and intergroup competitiveness.[52] As the policy environment has become more open, the possibility for competition between intergovernmental and other groups increases. These changes may affect the lobbying activities of the state and local interest groups.

Since the decentralizing tendencies of the decrease in federal grants have created a tension between the spatial concerns of the government groups and the functional concerns of the other interest groups, state and local groups may have difficulty joining together in a coalition during the fourth phase of intergovernmental lobbying. Increased competition for scarce funds is an incentive for the groups to distance themselves from each other.

IMPACT

Measuring the impact of interest groups is extremely difficult. Because so many variables are involved in the creation of policy (timing, public opinion, administration support, congressional and committee support, fiscal problems as well as interest group input), it is difficult to determine which variable had the most impact on any particular legislation or policy. Indeed, even if one were able to determine that "interest groups" were the decisive variable, it would still be difficult to decide which interest group had the most impact. "There is relatively little influence or power in lobbying per se. There are many forces in addition to lobbying which influence public policy; in most cases these other forces clearly outweigh the impact of lobbying."[53]

Nevertheless, there have been several attempts to evaluate the impact of interest groups on particular policies. Group impact, or success, is generally defined by whether the group achieves desired policies in areas in which it lobbied. A group is successful on a particular policy if its access to decision-makers results in achievement of its goals; and a group is successful in general if it has a high ratio of goals won to goals lost.[54] Although Raymond A. Bauer et al. found the business lobby to be ineffective in influencing congressional decision-making in foreign trade policy,[55] many groups have been successful in their policy endeavors. The elderly and women's groups are just two examples of interests that have lobbied for and achieved legislation favorable to their groups' goals.[56] State and local interest groups had their share of success in the second and third phases of lobbying, including urban mass transit and housing programs, revenue sharing, and federal assumption of public assistance costs.[57]

Because it is so difficult to discern the exact impact of any particular actor in a policy area, studies of group impact have generally concentrated on the factors that are most likely to lead to success. Such factors include the scope of the policy, the other actors involved, and the groups' own resources. Groups tend to be more successful on narrow, specific issues rather than broad ones; they are more successful in keeping the status quo than in changing it, and successful changes come incrementally rather than comprehensively.[58] Groups are also more successful when other groups support their position: consensus and the formation of coalitions increase the possibility for policy achievement. When conflict does exist, contacts with committee staff make "the biggest difference for the group."[59] Finally, the internal resources of a group—including its professional staff, its funds and its members—can affect its lobbying success. State and local groups have fewer monetary resources than some other groups, but they are effective at exhorting their members to action and have competent professional staff.[60]

State and local government groups established themselves as important lobbying organizations under the War on Poverty; Nixon encouraged their participation in his New Federalism. In contrast, Reagan saw little distinction between intergovernmental lobbies and other lobbies, and his New Federalism, developed independently of them, did not receive a warm reception from the state and local groups.[61] When Haider's study was published in 1974, the political environment was favorable to these groups. The budget deficit and new conceptions of intergovernmental relations created a more negative political environment. State and local lobbies have been shown to have an impact in a political environment in which federal funding to subnational governments is increasing. The time period of this study (the 100th and 101st Congresses) followed a phase of decreased domestic spending. When federal resources are scarce, how well do subnational governments fare? This book examines the impact of the groups in a period of fiscal restraint.

CONCLUSION

State and local groups are in some ways very similar to other interest groups. They attempt to gain access to the national government for the purpose of influencing policy. Their influence, like that of other groups, rests on their ability to communicate information, and their tactics of communication are similar to those of other groups. State and local interest groups sometimes act in coalitions with one another and with other groups. Although it is difficult to measure the impact of any interest group, state and local groups have had success, as defined by policy outcomes favorable to the desires of the groups.

State and local interest groups differ from other interest groups in significant ways. Most importantly, their membership consists of public, elected officials, which gives them increased access. It is difficult to classify them as either private or public interest groups, for while they are not private, their aims do not necessarily coincide with the idea of a "collective good." State and local governments, above all else, wish to maintain their status and authority vis à vis each other and the national government. As such, their interests revolve around functional (geopolitical) as well as substantive (policy) lines.

The previous study of state and local interest groups found them to be effective when the federal grant system was expanding. This work reexamines the state and local groups during a time when the federal grant system was contracting. The lobbying tactics and success of the government groups may be different in the current time period. Although the spatial interests of the state and local groups are unlikely to change, their ability to realize those interests may be very different in the current time period than during the period of Haider's study.

The next three chapters analyze the cases chosen for study (the Act for Better Child Care, the Family Support Act and the National Affordable Housing Act) by examining the tactics of the government groups and the perceptions of congressional and association staff of their effectiveness. The final chapter looks at the overall influence of the groups on the three acts, expanding on Haider's study by placing the legislation in the economic and political context of the fourth phase of intergovernmental lobbying.

NOTES

1. James Madison, *Federalist 10*.

2. The "Big Seven" state and local interest groups also includes the International City Managers Association (ICMA) and the Conference of State Governments (COSGO), which are not included in this study because they are technically not lobbying organizations, a fact borne out by comparison of the groups' frequency of testimony. The five groups mentioned testified at least

two hundred times each between 1979 and 1989, while the other two groups testified less than fifty times. See Hays, "Intergovernmental Lobbying, " pp. 1084–1085.

3. David Truman, *The Governmental Process* (New York: Knopf, 1951).

4. Theodore Lowi, *The End of Liberalism* (New York: W.W. Norton and Co., 1979).

5. E. E. Schattschneider, *The Semisovereign People* (New York: Holt, Rhinehart and Winston, 1960).

6. Jeffrey Berry, *The Interest Group Society* (Boston: Little, Brown and Co., 1984).

7. Graham Wootton, *Interest Groups: Policy and Politics in America* (Englewood Cliffs, N.J.: Prentice-Hall, 1985), pp. 54–55.

8. Truman, *The Governmental Process*, p. 506.

9. Haider, *When Governments Come to Washington*, p. 229.

10. Ibid., p. 306.

11. Lewis Anthony Dexter, *How Organizations are Represented in Washington* (Indianapolis: The Bobbs-Merrill Co., Inc., 1969), p. 122.

12. Suzanne Farkas, *Urban Lobbying: Mayors in the Federal Arena* (New York: New York University Press, 1971), p. 28.

13. Lester W. Milbrath, *The Washington Lobbyists* (Chicago: Rand McNally & Co., 1963).

14. Ibid., p. 9.

15. Jeffrey Berry, *Lobbying for the People* (Princeton: Princeton University Press, 1977), p. 7.

16. Haider, *When Governments Come to Washington*, p. 89.

17. Farkas, *Urban Lobbying*, p. 26.

18. Haider, *When Governments Come to Washington*, pp. 161–171.

19. Ibid., pp. 223–224. See also Farkas, *Urban Lobbying*. She differentiates between substantive (policy) interests and functional (geographic) interests. (Farkas uses *substantive* where Haider uses *functional*, and *functional* where he uses *spatial*.)

20. Jack Walker, "Origins and Maintenance of Interest Groups," *American Political Science Review* 77 (1983): 390–406.

21. Farkas, *Urban Lobbying*, p. 6.

22. Haider, *When Governments Come to Washington*, pp. 88–90.

23. Conlan (*New Federalism*, pp. 110–111, 158–160) suggests that Reagan's attempt to reorganize federalism represented more than a desire to give responsibility back to the states. It was also part of a larger plan to "defund the left."

24. Truman, *The Governmental Process*.

25. Robert Salisbury, "An Exchange Theory of Interest Groups," *Midwest Journal of Political Science* 13 (February 1969): 1–31.

26. Peter B. Clark and James Q. Wilson, "Incentive Systems: A Theory of Organizations," *Administrative Science Quarterly* 6 (September 1961): 129–166.

27. Mancur Olson, Jr. *The Logic of Collective Action* (New York: Schocken Books, 1970).

28. Milbrath, *The Washington Lobbyists*, p. 20.

29. Berry, *Lobbying for the People*.

30. Milbrath, *The Washington Lobbyists*, p. 41.

31. Diana M. Evans, "Lobbying the Committee: Interest Groups and the House Public Works and Transportation Committee," in *Interest Group Politics*, ed. Cigler and Loomis, pp. 258–259.

32. Haider, *When Governments Come to Washington*, pp. 93–94.

33. Ibid., p. 98.

34. Ibid., p. 69.

35. Farkas, *Urban Lobbying*, p. 172.

36. Ibid., pp. 180–181.

37. Haider, *When Governments Come to Washington*, p. 256.

38. Milbrath, *The Washington Lobbyists*, p. 229.

39. Haider, *When Governments Come to Washington*, pp. 241–244.

40. Ibid., p. 15; Farkas, *Urban Lobbying*, p. 112.

41. Haider, *When Governments Come to Washington*, p. 37.

42. Sabato, *Goodbye to Good-time Charlie*, pp. 174–175.

43. Farkas, *Urban Lobbying*, pp. 103–105.

44. Carol S. Greenwald, *Group Power, Lobbying and Public Policy* (New York: Praeger, 1977), p. 330.

45. Truman, *The Governmental Process*, pp. 366–367.

46. David Knoke, *Organizing for Collective Action: The Political Economies of Association* (New York: Aldine De Gruyter, 1990), p. 19.

47. Haider, *When Governments Come to Washington*, pp. 184–196. The governors were eventually successful in adding amendments that increased the states' role. A similar grouping occurred around the Juvenile Delinquency Prevention and Control Act of 1968, but the mayors emerged victorious.

48. Ibid., p. 75.

49. Ibid., p. 215.

50. Farkas, *Urban Lobbying*.

51. Hugh Heclo, "Issue Networks and the Executive Establishment," in *The New American Political System*, chapter 3, ed. Anthony King (Washington: American Enterprise Institute for Public Policy Research, 1990).

52. Allan Cigler and Burdett A. Loomis, "Organized Interests and the Search for Certainty," in *Interest Group Politics*, 2nd ed., chapter 18, ed. Cigler and Loomis, p. 388.

53. Milbrath, *The Washington Lobbyists*, p. 354.

54. Greenwald, *Group Power*, p. 327.

55. Raymond A. Bauer, Ithiel de Sola Pool, and Lewis Anthony Dexter, *American Business and Public Policy* (Chicago: Aldine-Atherton, Inc., 1972).

56. See Joyce Gelb and Marian Lief Palley, *Women and Public Policies* (Princeton: Princeton University Press, 1987); also Christine L. Day, *What Older Americans Think* (Princeton: Princeton University Press, 1990).

57. Haider, *When Governments Come to Washington*, p. 212; Farkas, *Urban Lobbying*, p. 247.

58. See Dexter, *How Organizations Are Represented in Washington*, and Truman, *The Governmental Process*.

59. Evans, "Lobbying the Committee," p. 272.

60. Haider, *When Governments Come to Washington*; Farkas, *Urban Lobbying*.

61. Conlan, *New Federalism*, p. 224. See also Reed, "The Changing Role of Local Advocacy," and Levine and Thurber, "Reagan and the Intergovernmental Lobby."

Chapter 3

The Politics of Coalition-Joining: Child Care Legislation

Child care legislation was passed in the 101st Congress as provisions of the 1990 budget reconciliation bill, P.L. 101-508. The provisions included both a grant program to states for delivery of child care services and an extension of the Earned Income Tax Credit (EITC) for parents with children.[1] The legislation marked the culmination of a process that had begun three years earlier, when Democrats proposed the Act for Better Child Care (ABC), a new federal grant program. In response, Republicans had proposed competing legislation to assist parents through tax credits. Rather than choosing between the two alternatives, Congress eventually combined them in the budget bill. Prior to enactment, child care legislation was the subject of a jurisdictional battle in the House between the Ways and Means and the Education and Labor Committees, a rift between a liberal advocacy group and two Democratic Representatives, and a debate over the separation of church and state.

Throughout the process, state and local groups played a mostly behind-the-scenes role. However, the National Governors' Association was visible at several points in the process. Governors William Clinton (D-AR) and Thomas Kean (R-NJ), the "lead governors" on the child care issue, were vocal supporters of both the grant and tax proposals, and they and other governors publicly expressed their concern over the establishment of national standards for child care. The NLC released a survey in 1989 of the nation's cities that listed child care and housing as their primary concerns.[2] Each of the five state and local groups also testified at congressional hearings on child care. Outside the public eye, staff members of the NGA assisted in forging compromise on the legislation, and the NCSL provided congressional staff with an analysis of the various child care proposals. Staff from each of the groups also lobbied individual members of Congress.

The NGA and NCSL were eventually successful in their efforts to have Congress delete the portion of the grant program that would have established national standards for child care providers. Newspaper coverage of the child care legislation credited NGA with eliminating requirements for national standards. NCSL also actively lobbied for a new grant program rather than an expansion of Title XX funds earmarked for child care; the final legislation was consistent with the group's preferences on this issue. The local groups were somewhat disappointed that funding for child care was funneled through the states rather than delivered directly to localities. Overall, however, both state and local groups were pleased that a grant program was established, regardless of its funding mechanisms. The state and local groups did not bring child care to the congressional agenda, but once the issue was considered in Congress, their active involvement affected specific provisions of the legislation as passed.

AGENDA-SETTING

Background

Congressional involvement in child care for working mothers dates to 1942, when Congress passed and the President signed the Lanham Act, which provided grants to states to pay for care of children whose mothers worked in wartime industries. When the war was over, the grants stopped. Almost thirty years later, in 1971, President Nixon vetoed a bill that would have provided child care to working mothers, calling the bill "anti-family." Nixon's concerns reflected the concerns of Americans in general, who feared institutionalized day care was a socialistic method of breaking family ties. Mothers were expected to stay home and take care of their own children rather than send them to group settings. "Many Americans are old enough to remember a time when day care was regarded as a communist plot. Only a nation with brainwashing on its agenda would allow its children to be turned over to strangers to raise."[3]

Since 1971, the percentage of women in the workforce has steadily increased. The number of two-parent families has declined, and in many such families both parents work. In single-parent families, the caretaker parent also often works. As a result, more children are placed in day care. Child care is now generally accepted as necessary, although many individuals still fear federal involvement. Reflecting these ambivalent attitudes, federal policy toward child care has been rather piecemeal. The Head Start program, passed as part of the Social Security Act of 1965, provides educational services to pre-school children from disadvantaged backgrounds. Although technically not a child care program, Head Start eliminates the need for some low-income mothers to find day care for pre-school age children. Title XX of the Social Security Act, the Social Services Block Grant (SSBG, passed in 1974), provides funding for services including child care to low-income mothers. A set-aside for child care was cut from the SSBG in 1981. Congress passed a child care tax credit in 1976 and expanded it in 1981. Also in 1981, Congress passed legislation giving a tax credit to employers that provide child care for employees.

The Problem Stream

In the 1980s, the lack of child care, particularly for low-income mothers, was perceived as a problem. As the number of working women with children increased, the fears of socialized child care diminished. In 1984, the House Select Committee on Children, Youth and Families, chaired by George Miller (D-CA) released a report (H. Rpt. 98-1180) that examined child care, noting in particular the problem of children with no after-school care (the so-called "latch-key children") and the variation of standards and quality of care among states. The House passed a bill in 1984 to encourage local after-school programs; the bill died in the Senate. Both the House and Senate proposed legislation in 1986 that would have expanded Title XX funding for child care and improve standards for provision of child care. Again, the legislation died.

The problems with child care legislation were mainly partisan. Democrats wanted to increase federal grants for child care. Republicans, particularly the Reagan administration, were opposed to increasing federal involvement. Throughout the mid-1980s, child care was on the Democratic congressional agenda. It did not get to the top until 1988. That year, after a Democratic push, Republicans also became more active in the issue and child care became a top priority for both parties.

What happened in 1988 to push child care to the top of the congressional agenda? Advocacy groups and Democratic legislators had been interested in the issue for years but had experienced little success. Why did child care suddenly become a high priority issue in 1988? The answer may be found by applying John Kingdon's model of the agenda-setting process. Kingdon says that ideas reach the policy agenda when each of three "process streams" (problem, policy and politics) are joined together in a "policy window" of opportunity.[4] For child care legislation, 1988 was the year that these three streams came together, although final legislation was not passed until two years later.

Kingdon's problem stream is the method by which a particular problem comes to the attention of policymakers. There are several ways that a problem may be identified: by a "focusing event," a crisis or disaster that directs attention to the issue; by systematic indicators such as statistics or research findings; and by feedback from government agencies that a particular program is not working well. The child care problem became a subject of concern primarily by systematic indicators. There was no focusing event in child care.

Although some may have considered the lack of adequate child care to be of crisis proportions, the situation had evolved gradually and there was no single event that pointed to child care as a problem.

However, there were systematic indicators that the supply of child care was inadequate to meet the demand for it. For example, according to the Bureau of Labor Statistics, the percentage of working women with children under six was 56.7 in 1987, up from 40.9% ten years earlier. And, while there were more than ten million children under six with working mothers in 1984, there were fewer than three million licensed day care slots. In addition, public opinion polls conducted by children's advocacy groups indicated that a majority of Americans viewed child care and children's issues as areas in which the federal government should be more involved.[5]

Systematic indicators were communicated to Congress in other ways as well. Since there was no comprehensive federal program for child care, feedback came from the states and localities, which were experiencing difficulties in providing child care services. Kingdon would classify this type of information as a systematic indicator, not feedback, since it was coming from state rather than federal programs. Congressional hearings on the subject of child care brought some state and local level problems to the attention of Congress in 1988. Parents testified that they could not afford quality day care and alleged abuse on the part of child care providers. Labor groups testified that day care providers received below poverty-level wages. Researchers testified that child care standards varied from state to state. And governors testified that they needed federal assistance to provide quality day care in their states, although their opposition to national standards ran counter to some of the reasons other groups were in favor of child care legislation.

Four governors testified at a Senate child care hearing in February, 1988[6]: New York Democrat Mario Cuomo, Minnesota Democrat Rudy Perpich (for the National Governors' Association), Michigan Democrat James Blanchard and New Jersey Republican Thomas Kean. All of the governors (and one former governor, South Carolina Democrat Richard Riley) testified in favor of a Kennedy proposal to expand pre-school education. Each of the governors already had a pre-school program in his own state. The governors' testimony emphasized the long-term benefits of such programs, including lower drop-out rates and better performance in school. Although the governors highlighted their successes, their testimony nonetheless pointed to some problems. The states perceived a need for federal money to improve child care, particularly for those states that could not afford to provide programs like the ones in New York, Minnesota, Michigan, New Jersey and South Carolina.

It is not unusual for Congress to turn to state and local groups for support on issues to which the administration is opposed. Haider found that in the 92nd Congress, when the Nixon administration was cutting domestic programs, members of Congress called on the state and local government groups for assistance in prioritizing and defending these social programs.[7] Similarly, while the Reagan administration remained opposed to many domestic initiatives, Congress turned to state and local groups, as well as others, to assist it in setting domestic priorities.

Another systematic indicator came from within Congress itself. The Family Support Act was passed in 1988. This welfare reform initiative (discussed in detail in Chapter 5) provided incentives for welfare recipients to work, including extended child and medical care benefits. Inadequate child care had been identified as a problem for low-income women during the consideration of the Family Support Act. After its passage, some members of Congress wanted to provide companion legislation that was aimed at helping the working poor stay off the welfare rolls.[8] Providing assistance with child care was one way Congress could help the working poor. Passage of one bill thus set the stage for passage of another.

In 1988, then, several factors led to the perception that there was a "problem" in child care. There was an increased need for child care because more women with children were working. While the number of working mothers with young children had been increasing over the course of several years, various groups communicated this need to Congress in 1988. Congress itself was beginning to place child care high on its agenda, and was willing to consider policy options that came before it. State and local groups were some of many voices expressing concern over the issue.

The Policy Stream

While the problem of child care was gaining national prominence, interest groups were developing proposals to address the issue. Child care legislation had been proposed in the years prior to 1988. In fact, in 1984 Congress passed and the President signed a child care bill (P.L. 98-558) authorizing $20 million in grants to states; the act was never funded. In 1986, Representative George Miller (D-CA), chairman of the House Select Committee on Children, Youth and Families introduced a bill to increase Title XX funding for child care and provide additional funds for improving standards and training child care workers. Similar bills were introduced in the Senate. The legislation died when the congressional session ended.

In 1988, one child care proposal came to the forefront. A coalition of interest groups led by the Children's Defense Fund (CDF) and known as the Alliance for Better Child Care (or ABC coalition)[9] had developed a policy that was known as the Act for Better Child Care (or ABC bill). Senator Christopher Dodd (D-CT) and Representative Dale Kildee (D-MI) introduced the coalition's ABC bill in November 1987. The bill was similar to the Miller proposal from

1986, except that it created a new grant program, rather than earmarking Title XX funds for child care.

The ABC bill became the major vehicle for discussion on the child care issue. According to several staffers, the ABC bill was drafted by the group and then proposed by members of Congress, creating a problem of ownership: the alliance felt more strongly about the ABC bill (H.R. 3660 and S. 1880 in the 100th Congress and H.R. 3 and S. 5 in the 101st) than did its congressional sponsors. Several congressional staff members noted that while interest groups often draft suggested legislative language, it is rare for legislators to propose legislation drafted entirely by outsiders. This happened in the case of the ABC bill, which respondents said belonged to the coalition, not to its congressional sponsors. Most of the congressional staff interviewed noted that the ABC coalition's allegiance to the ABC bill made compromise difficult, and one said that after the ABC experience members of Congress vowed "never again" to allow a situation in which interest groups had ownership over a proposed bill.

The heart of the ABC bill, as originally introduced, was a $2.5 billion grant program (over three years) to states for child care funding for low-income families. The bill also created a national commission to set child care standards. In addition, states would be required to use a portion of their grant money to expand existing programs, such as Head Start. The legislation specified the percentage of funds that would be allocated to the various provisions. Nearly every aspect of the bill became the focus for some controversy. Conservatives and state governments were opposed to the establishment of a national standards commission. Conservative groups such as the Heritage Foundation, the Eagle Forum and the Family Research Council were providing information to Congress in an informal coalition opposing the ABC coalition. Republicans in Congress and the administration favored a tax break for parents over expanding or creating grants. Some members of Congress wanted to expand existing child care entitlements rather than establish a new program. Finally, whether and how to provide funds to church-based child care centers presented a constitutional question over the separation of church and state.

All of the respondents interviewed credited the ABC coalition with bringing child care to the top of the congressional agenda. One respondent said that "the advocates played a key role early on, mobilizing people, getting a response." A congressional respondent said that "Marian [Wright Edelman] and the coalition put this together. Without them and [their] continued push, there wouldn't be a bill. Their grass roots support was unmatched." In the agenda-setting phase of the process, the state and local groups were not a part of the ABC coalition. The coalition was much more active and was able to get the attention of members of Congress. In the agenda-setting phase, groups with specialized policy expertise have the advantage over government groups, which are generalists. The specialists tend to be better established in an issue area, and are able to use their public policy expertise to press their claims.[10]

Congressional and association respondents identified the lead group in the coalition as the Children's Defense Fund, whose staff drafted the legislative proposal that became the ABC bill. The coalition worked closely with Democratic members of Congress including Kildee, Dodd and Miller. The ABC bill became the centerpiece of the Democrats' efforts to pass child care legislation. Senator Edward Kennedy (D-MA) also proposed a "Smart Start" program for universal early education and child care and his Committee on Labor and Human Resources held hearings on the proposal. Kennedy's proposal served as an early forum for debate, thus contributing to the policy stream, but it was soon overshadowed by the debate over the ABC bill.

The Republicans also offered their own policy proposals. Labor Secretary Ann McLaughlin set up a task force to study the child care issue. The administration was opposed to a new grant program, but considered addressing the child care issue through the tax system. Vice President George Bush proposed an expansion of Head Start and a tax credit as part of his presidential campaign platform. In Congress, Senator Orrin Hatch (R-UT) and Representative Nancy Johnson (R-CT) introduced companion child care legislation (S. 2084 and H.R. 4002). The Republican legislation created a $250 million block grant program and established a liability insurance pool for day care providers. Although the Republican bill had a significantly lower price tag than the Democratic bill, its very existence signified a Republican willingness to address the child care issue through a new grant program. More importantly, Senator Orrin Hatch (R-UT) agreed to work with Senate Democrats to develop a compromise bill. Hatch's involvement with ABC was crucial because it was the first indication of a possible bipartisan consensus on the child care issue.

Although the state and local groups were not a part of the ABC coalition in the beginning, state groups played some role in policy development. Governors representing the NGA testified at hearings on the child care issue. While the ABC coalition had initially identified lack of uniform standards as a major area of concern, the NGA early on registered its opposition to any type of national standards, stressing instead the need for state "flexibility" to set their own standards. The issue of national standards later became a subject of some debate, but at this point it was just one more ingredient in Kingdon's "policy primeval soup." In 1988 the policy options in this "primeval soup" consisted of proposals to create new grant programs for child care, to expand an existing program (Head Start), to provide for universal early childhood education and to provide child care tax credits. In addition, although it had been unsuccessful in 1986, a proposal to expand Title XX child care funding was still a possibility.

The Political Stream

Perhaps the most important factor in placing child care at the top of the legislative agenda was that 1988 was a presidential election year. A change in administration could only help the passage of child care legislation. The "Reagan administration . . . structured the governmental policy agenda to include items on which it placed a high priority, but in the process made it virtually impossible to get other potential initiatives seriously considered."[11] Child care was one of those potential initiatives. While Reagan had been opposed to the creation of new child care programs, a new administration might be more favorably disposed to such programs. In fact, both presidential candidates endorsed child care assistance as part of their campaign platforms. Democrat Michael Dukakis supported the concept of the ABC grant proposal (a similar proposal became part of the Democratic platform), while Republican George Bush proposed a refundable tax credit for low-income families with children and increased funding for Head Start. The two candidates were trying to woo different voters with their child care proposals. Democrats wanted to win back the middle-class voters who had defected to Reagan, while Republicans wanted to diminish the "gender gap."[12] Whatever the reasons for their support, once the candidates endorsed child care assistance, the issue achieved national prominence.

In addition to political elections, Kingdon identifies changes in the national mood and interest group pressure campaigns as factors in the political stream. The national mood was different in the late 1980s than it had been at the beginning of the decade. Reagan's campaign to get the government "off our backs" was fading from memory. The general public was more willing to let the government solve its problems. In addition, the attitude toward day care had been undergoing a gradual change. No longer considered a "socialist plot," child care was increasingly seen as a necessity for many families. Interest groups, especially the Children's Defense Fund, capitalized on this. According to at least one respondent, there was a great deal of media coverage of the child care problem, and CDF was primarily responsible for it.

Several factors in the political stream paved the way for child care legislation. Interest groups and the public were in favor of federal government involvement in child care. For example, a poll conducted for CDF and the American Federation of State, County and Municipal Employees (AFSCME) in June 1989 showed that 63% of the general public, and 59% of individuals who were not currently raising children, believed that the national government should become more involved in child care.[13] Even more important, the end of the Reagan administration opened the door for consideration of legislation to which Reagan was ideologically opposed. When both presidential candidates endorsed the concept of federal child care legislation, its placement on the agenda was ensured.

By the end of 1988, the problem, policy and political streams all were disposed favorably to child care. There was a general perception, among interest groups, public opinion and members of Congress, that child care was a problem that the federal government should address. Interest groups (the ABC coalition) developed policy, congressional Democrats proposed it, and Republicans submitted counterproposals. The presidential candidates also participated in the "policy stream," and their attention to child care, combined with the public and interest group concern, placed child care in the political stream. The state and local groups played a relatively limited role at the agenda-setting phase. The NGA assisted in defining the problem by participating in the hearing process, and played a small part in the policy stream by opposing national standards. It is not unusual that the government groups played a small role at this stage in the process. Although the state and local government groups sometimes are responsible for placing new policy ideas on the agenda, they are hampered in this process by the fact that they have diverse membership and often have difficulty achieving consensus. Frequently, this diversity serves as an impediment to an initiator role for the groups.[14]

Since the NGA advocated a federal role in child care, it was one more group in the political stream whose support made child care legislation feasible. Although the state and local groups were not the primary force behind placement of child care on the congressional agenda, the NGA's unobtrusive, behind-the-scenes activities paved the way for its later ability to compromise, just as CDF's more strident, vocal tactics led later to a public dispute with Congress. As a congressional respondent put it, "the state and local groups know what it's like to be beholden to groups [so they] avoided taking a position. [The groups] could give the merits of either approach. Their interest was in simply getting the money."

POLICY FORMULATION

By the end of 1988, child care legislation had come to the top of the congressional agenda. A "policy window" was opened, presenting an opportunity for congressional action on the issue. A policy entrepreneur, the Children's Defense Fund (the lead group in the ABC alliance), was available to push for enactment of its pet proposal. In August of 1988, the House Education and Labor Subcommittee approved the ABC bill (H.R. 3660) and the Senate Labor and Human Resources Committee approved the Senate version (S. 1885). However, neither house passed child care legislation in 1988. The new Congress convening in 1989 reexamined the issue.

The government groups used various tactics to lobby for their preferences on child care. Haider identifies eight common tactics used by state and local interest groups:

1. Use access and get the matter on the agenda
2. Build coalitions—Form alliances
3. Nourish your allies
4. Exploit cleavages
5. Gear strategies to the legislative climate
6. Count heads and money
7. Research—Counterresearch
8. Grassroots efforts[15]

The government groups used each of these tactics to some extent in lobbying for child care legislation. For example, while the NGA was not the main voice in getting the issue of child care on the agenda, the group successfully used its access to make sure its major concerns were among the available policy alternatives. The following sections will describe congressional consideration of child care, emphasizing the lobbying tactics used by the state and local groups.

Battle in the Senate: The Issue of Standards

The most important issue for the state groups was the elimination of federal child care standards from the ABC bill. The original ABC legislation created a national advisory committee to set standards in such areas as group size, staff/children ratios, training, parental involvement and health and safety requirements.[16] The idea of "quality assurance" was very important to the child care advocates who initially drafted the legislation. Early testimony reflected this concern. One association staffer called the early hearings "dead baby panels," because of the large numbers of parents testifying about child abuse at unregulated day care centers. While conservatives denounced the standards contained in the bill, child care advocates defended them. According to Children's Defense Fund president Marian Wright Edelman, "If we can regulate zoos and nursing homes, surely we can provide minimum health standards for children."[17]

The National Governors' Association and the National Conference of State Legislatures, as well as Republicans in Congress and the Bush administration, were adamantly opposed to national standards. NACO supported standards only if they were adequately funded. The position of the state interest groups was that the creation of standards should be left up to individual states. The groups were concerned that the federal government would create new mandates without adequate funding. While some states, such as New York and California, already had standards in place that would match or exceed new federal criteria, others (e.g., Georgia and North Carolina) had relatively minimal requirements for child care. The NGA and the NCSL were unyielding in their position that these states should not have to bear the cost of meeting extensive new federal requirements. According to Governor Clinton, "While we recognize the need for well-developed child care standards, the regulation of child care has been, and should remain, a state responsibility."[18]

The state groups' opposition to standards was in conflict with the coalition's position. The government groups were concerned with protecting what Haider calls their "spatial" interests: the NGA and NCSL wanted to ensure that state governments, not the federal government, controlled child care standards, or, as one respondent said, "the governors didn't want their hands tied." The coalition, on the other hand, was more interested in "functional" or policy issues. The coalition's definition of good child care policy was twofold: to ensure quality child care by establishing national minimum standards, and to make child care more affordable and available. The state groups agreed with the latter goal, especially insofar as it meant increasing federal funds, but they could not agree with the idea of national standards. Their overriding concern was in protecting their turf, and national standards would mean ceding some authority to the federal government.

The government interest groups are generally more concerned with spatial interests than both Congress and other interest groups, which concentrate on functional issues. It thus becomes necessary for the government groups to "seek the imposition of spatial concerns on functionally oriented and structured institutions."[19] The groups often do this by phrasing their arguments in functional rather than spatial terms. However, in this case, the groups framed their position in a spatial context, perhaps because the political climate of the fourth phase of intergovernmental lobbying is favorable to state policymaking. The governors, in lobbying against national standards, stressed regional differences in the provision of child care and posited that better standards could be established by the states, which would know their own needs best. Governor Kean testified on behalf of the NGA that "uniform regulations would not account for differing regional needs. Day care is not like socks or pantyhose—one size doesn't fit everybody."[20] The administration was also opposed to the standards provision. In a letter to Senator Kennedy, signed by the secretaries of Treasury, Health and Human Services and Labor, the Bush administration maintained that it was adamantly opposed to national standards, which "would increase the cost of supplying child care."[21]

National standards for child care remained intact in the versions of the ABC bill approved by House and Senate Committees in 1988. The issue was revisited in the Senate when Senators Orrin Hatch and Christopher Dodd introduced S. 5, the 1989 version of the child care bill, in January of that year. Although S. 5 still included a federal standards commission, the commission would have greater state and local representation. This was a small legislative victory for the state and local groups, but it was not enough to satisfy the NGA and NCSL, which continued to put pressure on Congress to drop standards from the bill. Individual governors lobbied on behalf of the NGA. Several governors testified at committee hearings in 1989 declaring their support for the grant portion of the ABC bill while at the same time denouncing its provisions on standards. Kean and Governor Clinton, the "lead governors" for the NGA on the issue of child care,[22] sent a letter to Dodd in March 1989 requesting that standards be dropped. They also met with key congresspersons, and in June 1989 the NGA, Senate Republicans and the Bush administration reached a compromise with Senator Dodd: the national commission would remain in the bill, but the standards it set would be "recommended" rather than required. States would be required to set standards that they developed themselves.

The elimination of standards was the biggest "win" for the state groups in the child care bill. In order to ensure passage of the bill, the ABC coalition, which had originally listed standards as one of their primary goals for the child care bill, accepted the compromise. "The ABC Alliance supports the agreement reached by Senator Christopher Dodd (D-CT) with the National Governors' Association, which modifies ABC's original approach, which would have established national standards."[23]   Press reports of the issue credit the elimination of national minimum standards to the efforts of the NGA, which was supported in its efforts by the Bush administration. "Provisions requiring standards for child care services were scaled back to win support of the National Governors Association and similar groups."[24] Congressional and association staff also credited the NGA with eliminating standards from the bill. One respondent claimed that the "Governors played a very pivotal role. If the governors do not want standards in the bill, there are not gonna be standards in the bill and CDF . . . and the coalition, anxious to get a bill through, opted for the easy route." The elimination of standards was NGA's priority for the ABC bill, and the group and its members lobbied persistently and publicly on the issue. NCSL, NACO and USCM also took public stands against standards. NCSL and NACO worked with NGA on the issue. NCSL members also lobbied individual members of Congress. It is not surprising that the compromise on standards was worked out in the Senate, where representation is by state: almost all respondents agreed that the NGA is more influential in the Senate than in the House. One House staffer said "the governors worked their magic over there [in the Senate]." Once the Senate had agreed to compromise, the House agreed to its position on standards.

The governors used five of the eight tactics identified by Haider in lobbying for the removal of national standards from the bill. They used their access to "get the matter on the agenda." Beginning with the agenda-setting phase of the process, the state groups made known their position on standards. NGA, NCSL, and NACO had individual members contact congressional members. This worked particularly well for the NGA: according to several respondents, individual governors can have a strong impact on the Senators from their own states. NGA counted money, if not heads, in that they wanted to ensure they got funding without mandates. NGA, NCSL, NACO and USCM formed a loose alliance, which although not overtly competitive with the ABC coalition, provided a strong voice counterbalancing the coalition's calls for national standards. The NGA in particular nourished its allies through private meetings with Senators, and the state and local groups were willing to compromise to some extent. The groups worked with both liberal members of Congress, who were strongly committed to child care legislation, and with conservatives, who were opposed to expanding the federal government's role through the imposition of standards. They geared their strategies to the legislative climate: realizing that a partisan battle might endanger the passage of child care legislation altogether, the groups worked mostly behind the scenes.

Battle in the House: Child Care as an Entitlement Program?

Another major controversy emerged over the issue of whether to fund child care under the existing Social Services Block Grant (by earmarking Title XX of the Social Security Act for child care) or to create a new child care block grant. Along with the ABC coalition, NCSL, NACO, USCM and NLC were in favor of a new block grant, while NGA was the only group to support the Title XX approach. Proponents of Title XX earmarks argued that it would ensure funding for child care as an entitlement program. Opponents wanted to establish a new funding stream in the hope of gaining more money for child care. Underlying the debate was a jurisdictional issue: the Title XX program falls under the authority of the House Ways and Means Committee, while a new child care program would be controlled by the House Education and Labor Committee. "On the surface, the dispute appears to be about how to finance the programs. Beneath the surface, however, it looks like a fight over what committees are going to run the programs in the future."[25]

The Governors Lose Ground

The ABC bill created a new grant program instead of expanding Title XX. Nevertheless, House Ways and Means Committee Chair Dan Rostenkowski sent a letter to then-Speaker Wright in June 1988, requesting that the bill be referred to his committee, because it benefited welfare recipients, who are under Ways and Means jurisdiction.[26] The committee obtained referral of ABC in 1989, although the bill went first to the Education and Labor Committee, which has jurisdiction over child care legislation. Education and Labor approved H.R. 3 in June 1989. Although Education and Labor amended the original legislation slightly (for example, by adopting the Senate bill's language on the standards issue), the ABC grant program to the states remained practically intact. The reported bill was then referred to the Ways and Means Committee. Ways and

Means had already begun considering child care as part of its budget reconciliation package. The committee had approved increasing Title XX funds and earmarking the increases for child care. When Ways and Means Committee members considered H.R. 3, they dropped the ABC grant program and substituted the Title XX earmark. In addition, in a compromise worked out by Representative Tom Downey (D-NY, acting chair of the Ways and Means Subcommittee on Human Resources) and Miller, the Title XX grant was combined with a child care tax credit, an idea which Republicans supported.

The entire child care package (the Title XX earmark and the child care tax credit) was added to the Ways and Means Commmittee's budget reconciliation measure. Worried that the inclusion of the Title XX expansion in budget reconciliation would exclude consideration of the ABC grant program, the Education and Labor Committee appended their version of H.R. 3 to their own budget reconciliation bill. When budget reconciliation went to the House floor, Charles Stenholm (D-TX) and Clay Shaw (R-FL) proposed an administration-backed substitute that included Title XX, Head Start and tax credit expansions and no standards requirements, and had significantly less funding than either the Ways and Means or Education and Labor proposals.

The National Governors' Association then stepped into the debate. NGA director Ray Scheppach wrote a letter to Stenholm and Shaw in which he stated, "Only your bill is consistent with the governors' child care policy because it provides for a grant program that allows states the flexibility to tailor programs to meet their individual needs."[27] Although Scheppach had conferred with Clinton and Kean before writing the letter, Governor Clinton publicly stated that the letter did not reflect his views, and sent his own letter to Augustus Hawkins, Chair of Education and Labor, distancing himself from Scheppach's statement. Scheppach apologized for the NGA letter, saying that the word "only" was mistakenly inserted. Nine Democratic governors, however, signed another letter to Speaker Foley declaring that they disagreed with Scheppach's letter, with or without the word "only," and that they could not support Stenholm-Shaw because it did not provide enough funding for child care.[28]

According to one respondent, the governors "lost some ground" over the flap, and became somewhat less visible. The situation was embarrassing to the NGA, and "one or two people over there almost got fired over it." While the NGA was dealing with the problem internally, other state and local groups, particularly NACO and NCSL, became more actively involved with congressional staff. The incident was unusual for the NGA, which tends to go public only on issues on which it has internal consensus. The state and local groups are strongest in their lobbying abilities when their members are in agreement, but such consensus is difficult to achieve. "Whether acting as facilitators or initiators, they must first build internal consensus for action, which often raises insuperable problems."[29]

The ABC Coalition Causes a Stir

The Stenholm-Shaw amendment was ultimately rejected, and the House eventually approved a budget reconciliation package that included both the Title XX expansions and the ABC grant program. The House and Senate budget reconciliation bills went to conference committee, which deleted the Title XX expansion and retained Education and Labor's ABC block grant. In response, Representative Thomas Tauke (R-IA), supported by George Miller, among others, announced that he would propose an amendment instructing House conferees to delete the ABC block grant provisions from the budget reconciliation bill and replace them with the Miller-Downey Title XX earmark. The earmark would place child care under the jurisdiction of the Ways and Means rather than Education and Labor. To avoid the battle, the conference committee decided to remove child care provisions from the budget reconciliation bill completely, and House Speaker Thomas Foley announced that child care would have to wait until the following year. At this point, Marian Wright Edelman, president of the Children's Defense Fund, and spokesperson for the ABC Coalition, met with Foley to demand passage of child care legislation prior to Thanksgiving recess. Edelman also wrote a public letter to Downey and Miller, accusing them of waging a "private guerilla war" to obstruct child care passage. She claimed that they had proposed the Title XX earmark for "petty jurisdictional and power reasons."[30]

While the NGA's letter had been little more than embarrassing, Edelman's letter created an uproar. Congressional staff viewed Edelman's tactics as "overt hostility," and were angered that the CDF was attacking friends, Miller and Downey, who were liberal Democrats outspoken in their support of children's issues. Accounts of Edelman's meeting with Foley emerged, and some reports claimed that she had threatened the Speaker, a charge that Edelman denied. Although one respondent said that Edelman was probably right in her depiction of the motives of Downey and Miller (they were using obstructionist tactics to keep child care under the jurisdition of the Ways and Means Committee), respondents almost universally agreed that her outburst alienated congressional staff. Child care became a contentious issue, and former allies became enemies. One congressional staffer told of child care meetings that were scheduled without informing staff of key members of Congress who were considered to be "traitors" to the child care cause. Another claimed that CDF "made a lot of mistakes along the way."

Interestingly, the CDF's undoing paved the way for the state and local groups to increase their influence in Congress. As one respondent put it, "The advocates [the ABC coalition] played a key role early on, mobilizing people, getting a response. When CDF fell out of favor, the state and local groups took on the leadership role." Since the NGA was keeping a low profile, NCSL moved into the lead. NCSL, NACO and USCM were all opposed to the Title

XX expansions. CDF had created the battle lines, but the state and local groups moved in a less adversarial manner to stake their claim on the issue. This is a tactic that is common for the government groups: "As facilitators, the groups may exploit existing congressional cleavages to their own advantage."[31]

A congressional staffer noted that the difference between advocacy groups and the state and local groups is in their ability to compromise. "CDF staked out territory in which they would not compromise. [That] stifles us. They were too rigidly attached to the bill." Although this may not be entirely true (the coalition accepted the compromise on standards), the children's groups did appear to be more strident in their support of child care legislation. The state and local interest groups played more of a brokering role. On the issue of standards, the NGA was able to forge compromise without losing friends, in contrast to CDF's more argumentative tactics. Most respondents mentioned the importance of the governmental groups in forming compromise. Even when the NGA had a dispute, the governors and staff argued with each other and public letters were worded so as not to offend past or future allies in Congress. NGA's squabbles were internal; the coalition's were with members of Congress.

When Foley put off consideration of child care to 1990, the debate over the entitlement was delayed. When it came up again, CDF and the NGA were less visible than they had been in 1989. In contrast, the NCSL and NACO played a larger role than they had previously.

Upset with the bickering over the legislation in 1989, Foley insisted in early 1990 that the disputing committees come up with a compromise or the competing bills would face a floor vote on March 3. Foley's major concern was in getting a bill that could pass the House. The Title XX bill could do just that, but the ABC bill had wider interest group support.

> The problem for the leadership all along has been that while the Ways and Means plan is presumed to have broad enough support to pass the House, the Education and Labor bill has the backing of the broad array of interest groups that put the issue on the national agenda in the first place, particularly organized labor.[32]

Members of the two committees, afraid that a floor vote would create an opening for a Republican alternative, eventually decided to take the Title XX approach in exchange for keeping Education and Labor's Head Start expansions. Since the Senate had taken the ABC grant approach, the issue could be revisited in conference committee. When the compromise bill came up for a vote, Stenholm and Shaw again proposed their scaled-back alternative to the ABC bill. This time, the NGA stayed out of the debate, but NACO and NCSL fought against the Stenholm-Shaw amendment, which was eventually defeated.

NGA's official position was in favor of Stenholm-Shaw and the Title XX approach. However, in 1990 the organization did not lobby actively on this issue, probably because of internal division over it. Most congressional respondents could not remember what NGA's stand on the Title XX debate was. On the other hand, NCSL was on record in favor of S. 5 which took the block grant approach. According to a respondent, the group "was opposed to any bill that did not include a new grant program for child care." NCSL believed that a new grant would provide maximum funding for child care, and state legislators felt that the use of Title XX would bring too many strings (in the form of federal mandates) attached to the funds. While Congress members were aware that Title XX had a better chance of passing, the NCSL felt that ABC would be easier to implement. It is not clear why the NGA was in favor of Title XX, while other state and local groups were opposed. It may have been a question of pragmatism. While NACO and NCSL were holding out the hope that a new grant program would bring more money, NGA may have been resigned to the fact that appropriated money would be less than authorized, and wanted to guarantee funding through an entitlement program. This is not an unusual pattern. NCSL, as a group of legislators, was more focused on the political problem of getting the program passed, while the NGA, as a group of chief executives, was much more interested in the politics of administering the program.[33] While the bill was in conference, NCSL actively lobbied for the ABC program. The organization sent out a letter to key conference committee members, and an "action alert" urged NCSL members to write letters in favor of the ABC grant.

By the time the bill came out of conference, a compromise had been reached. The Title XX expansion was deleted. In exchange, the new bill had a small entitlement program for low-income families under Title IV of the Social Security Act, which fell under the jurisdiction of the Ways and Means Committee. The bill included a new grant, but it was renamed the "Child Care and Development Block Grant." Child care advocates got a new grant program, while the Ways and Means Committee got a program within its jurisdiction.

Although NCSL was lobbying actively against Title XX expansions, congressional staffers did not give the group full credit for the compromise, as they did for the NGA and standards. As one congressional staffer put it, "Everybody advocating for child care was opposed to Title XX." NCSL played a less visible role than NGA had on the issue of standards in the Senate. NCSL was not mentioned in most of the press coverage of the child care bill, while NGA was almost always credited with the compromise on standards. NCSL was, however, mentioned by almost all of the respondents as being influential in the passage of the legislation, and some respondents credit the NCSL with taking the lead when CDF fell out of favor and NGA lessened its pressure. NCSL's role was behind-the-scenes. The group provided information to congressional staff as well as other interest groups.

State and Local Tactics in the Title XX Debate

The NGA's staff letter to Representatives Stenholm and Shaw is an example of how not to act. First, the association should have taken no public stand until its members were in consensus. The NGA's letter and the Democratic governors' response to it indicated disagreement among individual members. In contrast, NCSL's mobilization of its own grassroots through its "action alerts" and state legislators' subsequent letters to Congress demonstrated agreement on the issue. Second, the NGA did not nourish its allies. By taking a strong stand in favor of a substitute bill, NGA risked alienating child care proponents in Congress. Clinton and other Democratic governors were quick to contact Democratic congressional leaders to smooth over any animosity engendered by the NGA's letter. While the NGA was allied with Republicans over the issue of standards, the group also needed to maintain the support of Democrats to ensure passage of a child care bill: "past alliances notwithstanding, the groups are not wed to either party exclusively, nor can they afford to be."[34]

The NCSL, on the other hand, used proven lobbying techniques. First, the group was able to exploit cleavages that had been forged by the coalition's dispute with members of Congress. The group consistently lobbied for a new grant program, but was seen as more willing to compromise than the ABC coalition. NCSL also formed an alliance with NACO and USCM, and the groups worked together to negotiate with congressional staff and members of Congress, carefully avoiding any conflicts with their congressional allies. An association staffer commented that "NGA was at the table, NCSL was at the door," meaning that while NGA was more visible in conferring with congress members, NCSL was providing background information. The group provided congressional staff and other interest groups with comparisons of the various child care proposals, and provided information on the states' ability to administer the various programs. The NCSL also relied on legislator-to-legislator contact: state legislators lobbied their congressional representatives personally. NCSL's overriding concern was the issue of money. According to a respondent, the association felt that the ABC grant program would bring the greatest amount of funds with the least amount of federal mandates. All of the group's activities were centered around that goal.

Other Issues

Tax Credit vs. Grants

Republicans and Democrats had competing approaches to child care. Republicans supported an expansion of the Earned Income Tax Credit, which would provide low-income families more money to spend on child care. The tax credit had the added advantage of assisting families in which one parent stayed home full-time to take care of the children. Democrats, on the other hand, wanted to increase supply by providing states with funding for child care programs. NCSL and NGA went on record in favor of both tax credits and a child care grant program. Although embracing both approaches may seem contradictory, most child care proponents favored such a plan in order to ensure presidential support of a child care bill. While the final legislation was in agreement with state and local preferences on this issue, their position was a means to an end rather than a legislative priority. Favoring tax credits made the bill more appealing to the administration, and the groups felt that this gave the legislation a better chance of passage. The groups did not lobby as actively for tax credit provisions as they did for the grant program and the elimination of standards.

Administrative Costs

The state and local groups' main concern was that the ABC money would not be attached to federal mandates. The creation of national standards was one mandate that the state groups opposed. As discussed above, they were in agreement with Republicans and the administration on that issue, which the NGA considered a win. But the groups were also concerned with the way in which the child care grants were allocated. The ABC bill determined the percentage of funds that would go to various activities. Three-quarters of the grants money was to assist families in paying for child care, 15% would be used for increasing the availability of child care, 10% would go to administrative costs. States felt that this was overly prescriptive. They were fearful of increased federal requirements for child care without enough federal money to fund them.

As passed, the child care provisions allow for 75% of the grant to be used for either direct services or to increase availability or affordability of child care, 5% goes to quality improvements, such as training or increasing salaries of child care workers, 18% to pre-school or before or after-school programs and/or early childhood development programs, and 2% can be used for various activities. The compromise was worked out between the Senate and the White House, which objected to what it viewed as the creation of a new child care bureaucracy in the original ABC bill. None of the respondents credited the state and local groups with the compromise, although at least one said their efforts helped. The state groups were uncertain as to whether the allocation was a win or a loss: they were happy that 75% of the funding was flexible, although they still felt the bill was overly prescriptive.

Vouchers

One of the biggest problems with child care legislation was the issue of how to provide assistance to church-based day care centers without raising the constitutional question of the separation of church and state. A significant amount of institutional child care is provided by religious-affiliated groups. One way to get around the problem was to provide funding through vouchers, which would go directly to individuals rather than to child care centers. Education associations were adamantly opposed to vouchers for child care, fearing that it might lead to the use of vouchers for public education. The state groups were also opposed to vouchers, because they wanted the funds to be funneled through government agencies rather than to be given directly to individuals, and they claimed that setting up a voucher system would be costly for state governments.

In order to maintain the support of religious groups, and to appease conservative critics of the child care legislation, child care conferees agreed to require that states give parents the option of using vouchers to pay for child care. This issue was NGA's and NCSL's biggest loss. Members of Congress knew that their compromise with NGA on standards had achieved the association's support of the child care bill, and, despite NGA's objections, they needed to use vouchers to gain the support of other groups, conservative members of Congress and the administration.

Local Issues

With the exception of NACO, the local groups played a much less visible role than the state groups on the child care issue. They were in favor of child care legislation in general, and were not strong in their position on most issues. However, they were in favor of child care advisory councils, which, in the original bill would have involved local governments in the child care planning process.The USCM had testified that "local officials should be included . . . on the national level in the advisory group that is mentioned in your legislation, so that local needs will be taken into account."[35] In addition, USCM, NACO and NLC were in favor of a pass-through provision that would have given large cities the ability to participate in the child care program if their states opted not to participate. Neither the advisory councils nor the pass-through provisions made it to the final bill. In order to make child care provisions more acceptable to the White House, Congress found it necessary to eliminate aspects of the bill that seemed to create a new bureaucracy. Thus, the local groups lost on the two provisions that were most important to them.

The local groups relied mostly on testimony to convey their positions. For example, the mayor of Hartford, Connecticut testified before Senator Dodd's (D-CT) subcommittee. The local groups had a much lower profile than the state groups; with the exception of NACO, they let the ABC coalition or the other government groups speak for them on most issues other than the pass-through provisions and local advisory councils.

LEGITIMATION

When the child care conference committee agreed on child care provisions in October 1990, the provisions were attached to budget reconciliation, a "must-pass" bill. The ABC grant program was replaced with the "Child Care and Development Block Grant," which was essentially the same thing under a different name. The House had voted to instruct its conferees to reject the ABC grant program, so the conferees renamed it. The grant required states to set their own standards and offer parents the option of using vouchers. In addition, child care provisions included an expansion of the Earned Income Tax Credit and an entitlement program for child care under Title IV of the Social Security Act.

The fact that child care was passed at all was considered a "win" by the groups that were lobbying for it. Although not every group was happy with every provision, compromises forged among the House, Senate, administration and interest groups left just about everybody with something that they wanted. Obviously, many groups had an impact on the legislation. In particular, the ABC coalition, headed by the Children's Defense Fund, was instrumental in getting child care on the congressional agenda. Every respondent mentioned the ABC coalition as being a vital force for the legislation. The coalition was credited with maintaining media coverage of the issue, convincing a large number of both liberal and conservative members of Congress (270 in all) to sign on to the legislation as co-sponsors, and keeping child care at the top of the agenda. A congressional respondent characterized their involvement as follows: "Clearly the Children's Defense Fund [was the impetus for the legislation]. Once they had it, they never let it go. They led a very aggressive, high-profile attack. . . . Everyone else pales." The ABC coalition also had a large network of state alliances that provided information and kept up grassroots pressure on individual members of Congress.

Respondent Perception of Impact

In order to determine the influence of the various groups on the child care legislation, congressional and association respondents were asked to list groups which they thought had a significant impact on the legislation and to rate the impact of those groups (and any state and local groups they did not mention) on the legislation. A score of 10 meant that the group had a very high impact;

Table 3.1 Ratings of Interest Group Impact on Child Care Legislation

Children's Defense Fund/ABC Coalition	7.8
National Governors' Association	7.4
National Conference of State Legislatures	6.1
National Association of Counties	4.4
National League of Cities	2.7
U. S. Conference of Mayors	2.0

Scores are averages of respondents' ratings of interest group impact. "10" means very high impact; "1" very low impact.

1 meant very low impact. Table 3.1 lists the average scores for CDF/ABC alliance and the state and local interest groups. CDF/ABC received the highest score. Almost every respondent said that the bill could not have passed without the ABC Coalition. Many respondents noted that the alliance did not get everything it wanted. Several said the groups accepted a very "watered-down" bill. Despite the fact that the alliance accepted a compromise on the issue of standards, which was one it its most important goals, respondents credited the coalition with forcing child care to the top of the agenda and keeping pressure on members of Congress to pass it. Even respondents who were somewhat bitter toward CDF and the ABC coalition still gave the alliance a high rating. Some respondents qualified their opinions by saying that the ABC/CDF would have received a lower rating later in the process, after the group had made congressional enemies. Nevertheless, respondents seemed to differentiate between "impact" and specific group preferences. Clearly, the ABC coalition did not achieve everything it wanted on the child care bill. Respondents gave the coalition its rating based on their perception of whether a bill could have been passed without it.

The National Governors' Association also received a very high score. This is due in large part to the asssociation's role in the standards compromise. In addition, several respondents noted that without the governors' support, legislation such as the grant program to the states could not get passed. The views of many congressional staffers are reflected in the statement of one: "You really can't accomplish very much if the governors . . . oppose what you're doing." While CDF and the ABC coalition were the impetus for getting child care legislation on the agenda, the NGA had the ability to act as a check. If the NGA did not support the legislation, it would have been difficult to pass, regardless of the coalition's tactics.

The NCSL has the third highest rating of the interest groups. Congressional respondents were generally less specific in their discussion of NCSL's role than were association respondents, but almost all agreed that NCSL was important in passage of the legislation. Their most important role was that of providing information. Respondents did not credit NCSL with specific legislative provisions as they did NGA or CDF's ABC Coalition, but they nonetheless felt NCSL was important.

NACO received less credit than NCSL. Most congressional respondents could not remember specific positions that NACO took on the legislation, but they did recall that NACO was involved in some of the negotiations. Congressional and association respondents attributed importance to NACO mostly because of its participation in coalitions, with CDF as well as with other state and local groups. The two other local groups were ranked much lower than the state groups and NACO. Many respondents felt that the two groups simply were not involved in the legislation. Some respondents mentioned the local advisory commissions and the local pass-through provisions as issues for which these two groups lobbied. Since these provisions did not pass, most respondents felt the groups had very little impact. Those respondents who said USCM and NLC had impact attributed it mostly to their participation in coalitions.

Group Positions on Specific Provisions

Since the respondents tended to assess the impact of various groups based on their success on particular provisions, it is interesting to examine how each group fared on the positions on which it took a stand. Table 3.2 lists the major provisions of the legislation as passed, and the final provisions were consistent with the state and local groups' and the ABC coalition's lobbying positions. If the legislation is a partially consistent with the groups' lobbying position, it will be counted as a win. For example, the administrative costs issue is a "win" for NGA and NCSL and the standards issue is a "win" for NACO (since, according to respondents, the final legislation moved more in the direction of what the state and locals wanted), the NGA had 3 wins, 2 losses; NCSL had 4 wins, 1 loss; NLC, 2 wins, 1 loss; USCM, 2 wins, 1 loss; NACO, 3 wins, 1 loss; and CDF, 3 wins, 1 loss. In rank order, then, NCSL had the best ratio of wins to losses, followed by NACO and CDF (tied), NGA, and USCM and NLC (tied).

Contrast that to the rank order according to respondent assessment of impact: CDF, NGA, NCSL, NACO, NLC, USCM. Clearly, respondent perceptions were based on more than simply whether the groups won on particular provisions. Most respondents seemed to take into consideration whether the legislation would have passed at all without that particular group's support. The respondents credited CDF with getting and keeping child care on the agenda and forcing action on a bill, even though the final legislation was not exactly what the group wanted. CDF was almost universally cited as the driving force

Table 3.2 State and Local Government Groups' Positions on
Legislative Provisions (Child Care)

	NGA	NCSL	NLC	USCM	NACO	CDF
National Standards	+	+	0	0	+/-	-
Grant Program	-	+	+	+	+	+/-
Vouchers	-	-	0	0	0	+
Local Issues	0	0	-	-	-	0
Tax Credits	+	+	+	+	+	+
Administrative Costs	+/-	+/-	0	0	0	0

\+ Provision is consistent with stated group policy
\- Provision is in opposition to stated group policy
0 Group did not take a strong lobbying position on this provision
+/- Provision is partially consistent with stated group policy on this provision

behind child care legislation, hence it got the highest rating based on the respondents' perceptions. Similarly, the NGA got the second highest rating, because respondents felt that if the group withheld its support, the bill would not be able to garner enough congressional support to pass.

It is interesting to note that NCSL is first-ranked based on its ratio of wins/losses and third-ranked based on respondent perception. NCSL is a much less visible organization than either CDF or the NGA. Its members tend to lobby their representatives without fanfare, and its major role is providing information. While NGA and CDF took strong public stands, NCSL kept up its direct lobbying tactics without much media coverage. It was not instrumental on the big compromises, but the group got more of what it wanted in the end. Perhaps this is because the NCSL is a large organization that is not dominated either by liberal Democrats or conservative Republicans: when the group reaches consensus on an issue, its position is more likely to be able to pass in Congress.

CONCLUSIONS

Haider makes a distinction between groups acting as initiators and groups acting as facilitators. While the distinction between the two roles is not rigid, in this case the ABC coalition was the initiator, while the state and local groups, particularly the NGA, were the facilitators. The ABC coalition proposed and pushed the legislation; the state groups assisted in forming compromise. In addition, the NGA, at least, acted in some ways as an obstructor: one congressional respondent said that the NGA "kept holding out the promise that they might [not] endorse the bill." The governors wanted to make sure their interests were taken into consideration as the legislation went through Congress. Another congressional respondent said that "the governors didn't block the bill once they got what they wanted," indicating that the NGA's primary power was its ability to block the legislation. This is a common tactic for the state and local groups. "The government interest groups withhold support or maintain an opposition posture to enhance their bargaining leverage in final outcomes."[36]

The child care act falls into Haider's second classification of congressional legislation: non-zero-sum legislation which can result in mutually acceptable compromises for the government interest groups. There was no fear of moving benefits from one level of government to another. Although the proposed ABC grant program would provide funds to states rather than localities, the local governments were not losing a program that had previously belonged to them. The local groups were not very involved in the legislation. Although they supported local advisory councils and pass-through provisions that failed, they were still content with the fact that there were new funds for child care.

The NGA and NCSL were aligned on all issues except the use of grants rather than expansion of Title XX. NGA stayed on the sidelines as Title XX was decided. Again, both groups were satisfied with the fact that new child care funds were going to the states, and they were pleased that the grants were not tied to national standards.

The groups used the eight tactics that Haider describes at various times in the process. All the groups nourished their allies, taking advantage of reciprocal relationships by not offending their supporters in Congress. The NCSL exploited cleavages when CDF caused congressional discord. The groups geared strategies to the legislative climate (such as the NCSL's "legislator-to-legislator" contact). They counted money by insisting that the legislation be adequately funded. The NCSL in particular used research to assist congressional staff in judging legislation, and the groups used grassroots efforts to ensure that members of Congress would hear from association members rather than staff.

NOTES

1. Under the legislation, states could use 75% of their grant money either to provide child care directly or to pay parents their child care costs. States were also required to provide before and/or after-school programs, early childhood development programs, or both. In addition, the provisions created a small entitlement program under Title IV of the Social Security Act, provided money for training child care workers, and gave parents a child health tax credit.

2. Spencer Rich, "Child Care, Housing Listed as Top Urban Priorities," *Washington Post*, August 29, 1989, sec. A, p. 3.

3. Jack Anderson and Dale Van Atta, "Time for New Ideas on Child Care, *Washington Post*, July 16, 1989, sec. B, p. 7.

4. John Kingdon, *Agendas, Alternatives and Public Policies* 2nd ed. (New York: HarperCollins College Publishers, 1995).

5. Julie Rovner, "Day Care Package Clears First Hurdle in the House," *Congressional Quarterly Weekly Report*, July 2, 1988, p. 1833, and Patrick L. Knudsen, "Committees Starting to Focus on Child Care," *Congressional Quarterly Weekly Report*, February 27, 1988, p. 514.

6. U. S. Congress, Senate, Committee on Labor and Human Resources, *Smart Start: The Community Collaboration for Early Childhood Development Act of 1988, Hearings*, 100th Cong., 2nd sess., 1988.

7. Haider, *When Governments Come to Washington*, p. 218.

8. Julie Rovner, "Congress Shifts Its Attention to the Working Poor," *Congressional Quarterly Weekly Report*, February 18, 1989, p. 326.

9. The coalition was made up of more than one hundred organizations, including labor groups, women's groups, children's groups (such as the Child Welfare League), and other non-profit groups.

10. Haider, *When Governments Come to Washington*, p. 226.

11. Kingdon, *Issues, Alternatives and Agendas*, p. 154.

12. Julie Rovner, "Both Parties Seek to Patch Gaps in Their Image," *Congressional Quarterly Weekly Report*, July 30, 1988, p. 2076.

13. Rovner, *Congressional Quarterly Weekly Report*, July 2, 1988, p. 1834.

14. Haider, *When Governments Come to Washington*, p. 214.

15. Ibid., pp. 228–254.

16. Rovner, *Congressional Quarterly Weekly Report*, July 2, 1988, p. 1833.

17. Quoted in Knudsen, *Congressional Quarterly Weekly Report*, February 27, 1988, p. 515.

18. Letter from Clinton to Sen. Packwood, March 14, 1989. Quoted in Julie Rovner, "Child Care Debate Intensifies as ABC Bill Is Approved," *Congressional Quarterly Weekly Report*, March 18, 1989, p. 587.

19. Haider, *When Governments Come to Washington*, p. 223.

20. U.S. Congress, Senate, Committee on Labor and Human Resources, *S. 1885, The Act for Better Child Care Services of 1987, Hearings before the Subcommittee on Children, Family, Drugs and Alcoholism*, 100th Cong., 2nd sess., 1988, p. 216

21. Rovner, *Congressional Quarterly Weekly Report*, March 18, 1989, p. 585.

22. The NGA appoints two governors (one Republican and one Democrat) to take the lead lobbying role on major legislative initiatives.

23. Marian Wright Edelman, "Pass That Child Care Bill," *Washington Post*, June 20, 1989, sec. A, p. 23.

24. Helen Dewar, "As Debate on Child Care Opens, Senators Agree on Goal but Diverge on Means," *Washington Post*, June 16, 1989, sec. A, p. 8.

25. Judy Mann, "Childish Performance on the Child Care Bill," *Washington Post*, November 22, 1989, sec. B, p. 3.

26. Rovner, *Congressional Quarterly Weekly Report*, July 2, 1988, p. 1836.

27. Quoted in Julie Rovner, "House Child Care Proposals Survive Floor Challenges," *Congressional Quarterly Weekly Report*, October 7, 1989, pp. 2639–2640.

28. Ibid., p. 2640.

29. Haider, *When Governments Come to Washington*, p. 218.

30. Quoted in Julie Rovner, "Delay on Child Care Measure Prompts Angry Criticism," *Congressional Quarterly Weekly Report*, November 18, 1989, p. 3162.

31. Haider, *When Governments Come to Washington*, p. 218.

32. Julie Rovner, "Long Deadlock on Child Care May Get Resolved Soon," *Congressional Quarterly Weekly Report*, March 10, 1990, p. 751.

33. See Haider, *When Governments Come to Washington*, p. 219.

34. Ibid., p. 239.

35. Testimony of Carrie Saxon Perry, mayor of Hartford, Connecticut, on behalf of the U.S. Conference of Mayors, U.S. Congress, Senate, Committee on Labor and Human Resources, *S. 1885, The Act for Better Child Care*, p. 59.

36. Haider, *When Governments Come to Washington*, p. 222.

Chapter 4

State and Local Bickering: Housing Policy

The National Affordable Housing Act became law on November 28, 1990. The legislation marked the first major federal initiative in housing policy since the Reagan administration. Like child care provisions passed the same year, the housing bill included both Republican and Democratic pet proposals. Housing and Urban Development (HUD) Secretary Jack Kemp was successful in his attempt to provide encouragement for low-income families to own homes, while Democrats succeeded in establishing a block grant that would deliver funds to states and localities for construction of public housing and housing assistance for middle-income families. Also like child care legislation, the housing bill was the product of more than two years' work and was based on recommendations developed by an umbrella organization made up of several groups.

There were significant differences, however, between the role of the outside organizations in congressional consideration of the two acts. The National Housing Task Force[1] was formed at the request of Senator Alan Cranston (D-CA), chair of the Senate Housing subcommittee, and funded by the federal government. The task force consisted of representatives from the housing industry, government groups and research organizations. It differed from the ABC coalition in that the focus of the task force was research rather than advocacy. The task force played a large role in the agenda-setting phase, as did the coalition, but unlike the coalition, the task force moved into the background once its report, "A Decent Place to Live," was presented to Congress. In addition, the task force's recommendations served as a rough outline of the housing bill, while the ABC coalition wrote the majority of the child care bill. The coalition's bill was introduced in both the House and the Senate; the task force's recommendations, while important to passage of the National Affordable

Housing Act, were somewhat diluted by Congress in comparison to the coalition's proposed legislation.

The state and local interest groups had much to gain from new housing legislation. First, it represented a significant source of money to the subnational governments. Representative Henry Gonzalez's bill (H.R. 1180) would have increased federal spending for housing by $7.7 billion in fiscal 1990. Second, it would relieve some of the stress placed on the state and local governments by the Reagan administration housing cuts. The less expensive Senate bill (S. 565, introduced by Senators Cranston and Alfonse D'Amato [R-NY]) would have created new programs to encourage public housing construction and provide incentives to middle-income home buyers. Such programs would partially assist in the homelessness problem and perhaps be a boost to state and local economies. Finally, housing legislation could give new sources of authority to the state and local governments. A counterproposal (S. 2504) by Senators Christopher Dodd (D-CT) and D'Amato would have consolidated nine housing programs into a block grant, giving state and local governments increased flexibility in the distribution of federal funds and the administration of housing programs.

Although the state and local groups could benefit directly from proposed legislation, they were less involved in the consideration of housing bills than in consideration of child care bills. The government groups did play a somewhat larger role in the agenda-setting phase of the housing process than in child care, and they were significantly involved in controversies over appropriations, but they were much less involved in consideration of the housing authorization. This may be because the state and local groups had more to gain, and, more importantly, less to lose, in the housing area than in child care. Each of the proposals being considered in Congress would have benefited state and local governments in some way; there was no proposal that entailed anything as onerous to state governments as the child care standards provisions. The state and local groups' primary involvement in the National Affordable Housing Act had to do with funding: how to split the percentage of funds going to the state and local governments respectively and, later, demands for full-funding of the authorizing legislation. In the former case, the state and local groups were pitted against each other, with the locals coming out ahead.

AGENDA-SETTING

Background

Throughout the 1980s, the federal government's involvement in housing policy substantially decreased. By the end of the decade, homelessness had increased dramatically, and home ownership among the young had fallen. Many

Democrats in Congress placed the blame for these two problems squarely on the Reagan administration, which had decreased federal housing expenditures by as much as 80% during its tenure. The end of the Reagan administration meant that there was a possibility for a Democratic president, and many in Congress felt that the time was right for a new housing policy. While the McKinney Homeless Assistance Act had been passed in 1987,[2] it was considered an emergency relief effort, and members of Congress hoped to pass additional legislation that would build on the McKinney Act and address the housing needs of low and moderate-income families as well as the homeless.

The relationship between the federal government and the subnational governments changed during Reagan's presidency. Reagan decreased federal expenditures for social programs such as housing, whereas in the 1960s Presidents Lyndon Johnson and Richard Nixon had cemented a partnership between the federal government and local governments by direct federal-local funding of such programs, in a relationship bypassing the state governments. In this atmosphere, local lobbies, such as USCM, became more powerful.[3] In fact, an entire urban policy subsystem developed around the increased amount of money being distributed to localities, particularly in the area of housing. This subsystem included the USCM, NLC, the National Association of Housing Redevelopment Officials (NAHRO) and advocacy groups such as Urban America and the Urban Coalition. Often, these groups were pitted against state interests, including the NGA (in the 1960s, the National Governors' Conference) and the Council of State Governments. The passage of the National Affordable Housing Act may represent a new stage in the development of the urban policy subsystem. While the state groups still had interests that diverged from the local and urban interest groups, all of the groups were brought together in an effort to increase federal funding for housing. Even NACO, which had not previously involved itself in housing issues, began to lobby in the area after the Reagan cuts of the early 1980s.

The Problem Stream

The problem stream for housing policy consisted mostly of systematic indicators. There was no "focusing event" to indicate an immediate crisis, and feedback was limited. Systematic indicators came from many sources, both within and outside of government. The NGA, NCSL, NLC and USCM all released reports and statistics that contributed to the problem stream. The most direct systematic indicator was a product of the Housing subcommittee (of the Banking, Housing and Urban Affairs Committee), whose chair, Senator Cranston, and ranking minority member, Senator D'Amato, set up the National Affordable Housing task force, which included representatives from advocacy groups, realtors' associations and mayors and governors. The task force submitted its report in March 1988. The report provided evidence that 36% of people aged twenty-five to twenty-nine owned their own homes in 1987, down from 44% in 1979. In addition, the task force reported that there was an 80% decrease from 1978 to 1988 in HUD funding for new housing, and that median rents increased at approximately twice the rate of median incomes between 1973 and 1983.[4] The task force was just the beginning. In response to its findings and recommendations, the Senate housing subcommittee held hearings on the National Affordable Housing Act in September 1988. James Rouse, chair of the task force, and David Maxwell, vice chair, testified at the subcommittee hearings, as did representatives of realtors' groups, low-income housing advocates and state and local interest groups. The USCM (represented by Jessie Rattley, mayor of Newport News, Virginia) testified that the rate of home ownership was declining in the U.S. and that low-income housing rents were at their highest level in twenty years.[5]

In January 1989, the National League of Cities released a survey blaming the lack of affordable housing for the decline in economic growth of cities.[6] That same month, the *Washington Post* published an article blaming the "housing crisis" on Reagan budget cuts. The article referred to a Census Bureau study, the American Housing Survey, which found that in 1985 half of all renters with incomes below the poverty level used 65% of their income for rent and utilities. More evidence of a housing problem came from a report released by the NGA and NCSL, which found that while the percentage of families owning their own homes (65%) had changed very little since the mid-1970s, owners were older in the 1980s: the home ownership rate for people under thirty-five declined by about 7% between 1974 and 1988.[7]

The housing problem cut across class lines. Not only were more and more low-income people finding it difficult to pay rent, young middle-income families were having difficulty coming up with down payments. In addition, the growing numbers of homeless people were an obvious sign of a housing crisis. "The availability of affordable housing has emerged as a powerful issue in recent years, politicians say, partly because of the growing visibility of the homeless and the complaints of middle class constituents who feel squeezed by the high cost of housing."[8]

Another systematic indicator came from already existing housing programs. Two potential crises came to the forefront in the late 1980s. The first crisis had to do with the stock of low-income housing. Between 1962 and 1973, housing developers signed contracts with the federal government to build low-income housing in exchange for subsidized mortgages, provided that the housing units remained low-rent for a period of time, usually forty years. The contracts also stipulated that owners could "prepay" the mortgages after twenty years and use the property for other purposes. About 360,000 of the 650,000 rental units built under this program would be eligible for prepayment between 1989 and 2005, with the bulk eligible in the years 1991 through 1994. The issue was how to "preserve" as many low-rent units as possible. Estimates of how many of these

360,000 units would be prepaid varied greatly, with HUD claiming 150,000 and the National Low-Income Housing Preservation Commission (formed at the request of Congress to study the preservation issue), 243,000.[9]

Related to the preservation issue was the expiration of federal rent subsidies. These subsidies are given to either owners or renters to offset the cost of rent for very low-income tenants. The subsidies, which were authorized in the mid-1970s, were appropriated for periods of as many as forty years. To renew those Section 8 subsidies scheduled to expire in 1991 would cost $23 billion.[10] If the subsidies were not renewed, a large number of tenants would not be able to afford their rent, and would face eviction from their housing units. Preservation and Section 8 issues were systematic indicators in Kingdon's model, not feedback. The information was obtained through monitoring of existing budgets, not implementation.

There was one focusing event that did not put housing on the agenda, but ensured that it would stay there. In May and June 1989, reports of widespread mismanagement at HUD prompted Justice Department and congressional investigations of the agency. HUD contractors were found to have embezzled at least $20 million, and regional offices as well as federal headquarters appeared to have neglected oversight of local offices. One local HUD employee was found to have diverted $1 million of government money to his own bank account. Another employee stole about $5 million of HUD money and gave it to the poor, earning her the nickname "Robin HUD."[11] The HUD scandal added to the perception that there was a crisis in national housing policy and kept housing on the national agenda. However, it in some ways inhibited the passage of affordable housing legislation, because HUD reform became a greater priority. [12]

By mid-1989, there was a general consensus among members of Congress, the media and interest groups that housing was a problem. Several systematic indicators had illustrated that problem to policymakers. The effect of the Reagan budget cuts, the increasing numbers of homeless people and the problems facing young, first-time, middle-income buyers were all communicated to Congress through various reports and studies, including reports by the NGA, NCSL, USCM and NLC. Members of some of these groups also participated in the National Housing Task Force. While the government groups were not the primary force at the agenda-setting phase, their voices were an important part of the process.

The Policy Stream

The task force report did more than define the problem. It also included specific policy proposals that became the basis for the National Affordable Housing Act (S. 565), introduced by Alan Cranston in the Senate. The task force proposed a "Housing Opportunity Program" (HOP) which would distribute $3 billion in the first year to state and local governments for the creation and renovation of low-income housing units. Each state would need to make a $1.5 billion match in order to qualify for the money. The report also suggested that HUD double the number of low-income housing units and that the Federal Housing Administration (FHA) decrease its requirements for down payments. In addition, to encourage private sector involvement, the task force recommended below market-rate loans to developers of low-income housing.

The state and local groups were somewhat active in the policy stream. NGA, USCM, NACO and NLC all had representatives testify at the initial hearings in September 1988 on the Rouse-Maxwell proposal for the National Affordable Housing Act. The NGA, which was in favor of the HOP program, testified that states were willing to become involved in a new housing policy, and were committed to spending new money for it. The NGA also went on record with their views of the relationship among the varying levels of government:

> It is important for the federal government . . . to avoid reverting to the historic direct relationship with local governments or public housing authorities that bypasses states and that disregards state and local government relationships. . . . It is not an approach that encourages state financial participation to any substantial degree.[13]

Unlike in the child care debate, there was no one governor advocating for housing legislation. Since it was not one of the group's priorities, no "lead governors" were named.

The U.S. Conference of Mayors testified that the HOP program was too complicated and should be made more flexible. The mayors also opposed the formula for distribution of HOP funds, 80% of which were to be divided 50-50 between state and local governments. USCM had its own policy alternatives to the National Affordable Housing Act. In February 1988, the Conference, the Lyndon Baines Johnson School of Public Affairs and the City of Austin, Texas, held a National Housing Forum. The final report from that forum, "Working Toward a Consensus," was submitted as part of the record in the hearings. Recommendations included a National Housing Block grant, funded at $4 billion per year and a $1 billion a year new housing production program.[14]

The representative from NACO testified in favor of the HOP program in concept, but the group was concerned about restrictions on using HOP funds for light to moderate renovation, and the 25% cap on the use of HOP funds for publicly owned housing. NACO also opposed the 50-50 split for the formula distribution of HOP:

> County officials recommend that the bulk of HOP funds that are to be allocated by formula be distributed to urban counties and metropolitan

cities in a manner analogous to the distribution of CDBG [Community Development Block Grant] funds. Although some states have developed exemplary housing programs, counties and cities, as the level of government closest to the people, have fervently moved to the forefront in addressing the housing needs of low and moderate income people.[15]

The National League of Cities also supported a flexible block grant approach, and wanted a larger percentage of the formula allocation to go to localities. In addition, George Latimer (mayor of St. Paul), testifying on behalf of NLC, called for full funding of the act when it got to the appropriation stage. Although NCSL did not send a representative to the Affordable Housing hearings, its joint report with NGA included some policy suggestions: individuals should be allowed to use IRAs for down payments, and state and local governments should continue to receive a tax exemption for mortgage bonds.

Cranston and D'Amato introduced their bill in March 1989. The legislation established a "HOME Corporation" in HUD to administer the $3 billion a year HOP housing construction program recommended by the task force. It also created an Office of Affordable Housing Preservation within HUD to examine the issue of expiring subsidies. States and localities would be required to submit five-year housing affordability plans, and the minimum FHA down payment would be lowered from 5% to 3%. First-time buyers could use money from IRAs for down payments. In addition, the bill extended the mortgage revenue bond and mortgage credit subsidies for first-time buyers. Despite the localities' concern about the split, the formula allocation would be divided evenly between state and local governments.

Gonzalez had introduced competing legislation in the House two weeks earlier. H.R. 1180 added $7 billion to the existing housing budget, including a new National Housing Trust Fund of $2 billion a year to subsidize first-time buyers' mortgage interest rates. While Cranston's bill created new housing programs, Gonzalez's simply reauthorized HUD and Farmers Home Administration (FmHA) programs. H.R. 1180 would add $7.7 billion to the existing annual housing budget, in contrast to the $4.1 billion increase proposed in the Senate legislation. In addition to the House and Senate approaches, the Bush administration had its own housing policy. HUD Secretary Jack Kemp favored enterprise zones and home ownership for low-income housing residents, and a greater emphasis on vouchers. All of these proposals were floating in the policy primeval soup by mid-1989.

The fact that dissimilar bills were introduced in the House and the Senate is an important difference between housing legislation and child care legislation. Senator Dodd and Representative Kildee both introduced the Act for Better Child Care, authored by the Alliance for Better Child Care. That bill became the basis for the child care debate, and, as noted in Chapter 3, the Alliance felt a great deal of ownership over the legislation, continuing to lobby actively for it throughout consideration. While the focus for the Senate debate was on the proposals made by the Rouse-Maxwell commission, according to a Senate staffer, "the House was on a completely different track." The debate was thus somewhat more diffused than was the child care debate. In addition, the Rouse-Maxwell commission was much more of a research group than a lobbying group. While the ABC coalition created the legislation and followed it, the Rouse-Maxwell commission simply researched and developed a policy proposal, but did not act as a lobbying group. Almost all of the housing respondents gave the Rouse-Maxwell commission at least partial credit for putting the housing problem on the agenda in the first place (although many credited Cranston's formation of the committee as the real impetus) and for development of a housing policy alternative. However, the commission was never mentioned in discussions of lobbying during consideration. According to a congressional staffperson, "The report was extremely influential and contributed to putting housing on the agenda. Once the bill went into Congress, there was a different set of players."

The Political Stream

While systematic indicators were bringing housing to the national agenda and Congress was developing policy alternatives, changes in the political climate were smoothing the way for passage of the National Affordable Housing Act. Three incidents were of particular importance in the political stream: the return of the Senate to a Democratic majority in November 1986, the 1988 presidential election, and the appointment of Jack Kemp as Secretary of HUD. The 1986 congressional election was important to housing legislation, because it gave the Democrats control of the Senate, enabling Senator Cranston to assume the chair of the housing subcommittee. Cranston was personally committed to housing legislation, and used his new position as the starting point. Several congressional respondents mentioned the importance of Cranston's position. One called it "the initial, direct impetus" for the placement of housing on the agenda; another mentioned Cranston's "strong personal commitment to housing," and the fact that Cranston was willing "to give the administration enough to keep them happy." Cranston assumed the chair in 1987, and after a housing bill failed to pass that year, he and D'Amato, the ranking minority member, put together the National Housing Task Force. Cranston became the "policy entrepreneur" to shepherd housing legislation through Congress.

The 1988 presidential campaign was also important to the passage of housing legislation. For one thing, it meant the end of the Reagan administration, which had been, in the words of a congressional respondent, "extremely hostile" to housing programs. Even if the Democrats did not win the presidency in 1988, it was likely that Bush would be more favorable to housing policy. But the Democrats in Congress were hopeful that Dukakis would win the presidency. In fact, according to several respondents, congressional Democrats felt that they were creating housing policy that might be implemented by a Dukakis administration. One of the members of the task force was Amy Anthony, the Secretary of the Massachusetts Office of Community Development, and a member of the Dukakis cabinet. Dukakis himself made housing a campaign issue, pledging to spend $3 billion over three years for nationwide low and moderate-income housing.[16] George Bush also used housing in his campaign, pledging to give aid to first-time buyers through FHA experiments with lower down payments, and insuring higher home mortgages.

Finally, once Bush was elected, he demonstrated his priority to housing policy by appointing Representative Jack Kemp as Secretary of the Department of Housing and Urban Development. Kemp, a proponent of "supply-side" economics, had several innovative ideas for housing policy, including "enterprise zones," low-income family home ownership, urban homesteading and vouchers.[17] Kemp kept a high profile during the debates over new housing legislation. In June 1989, he spoke at the U.S. Conference of Mayors meeting in Charleston, South Carolina, where he called on Congress to pass his proposals.[18] Although Kemp's home ownership programs were viewed negatively by Democrats in Congress (as well as the USCM, NLC, NGA and NACO), they created a bargaining point: eventually Democrats agreed to Kemp's home ownership program in exchange for his support of a block grant to encourage new construction.

By mid-1989, a series of factors contributed to placing housing policy on the congressional agenda. The Reagan administration had been a period of retrenchment for housing programs. By the time Reagan left office, the problem of homelessness and a decline in the percentage of young families owning homes created the impression of a housing crisis. The election of 1988 meant the inauguration of a president who would be more favorably disposed to housing programs. Cranston's assignment to the housing subcommittee chair created a policy entrepreneur, at whose request a task force was created to develop a new policy proposal. In addition, the imminent expiration of some federal housing programs created an opportunity for housing policy overhaul. The state and local groups participated in several aspects of the agenda-setting process. They were among the groups releasing statistics pointing to a growing problem in housing. Some of their members were represented in the Rouse-Maxwell Task Force. The USCM was a forum for Kemp's housing proposals. All of the government groups contributed to policy development by testifying at the Senate hearings on the task force report, which were held to find new ideas for affordable housing. The government groups were not the major players in the agenda-setting phase, but they had a significant voice.

The government groups may act as initiators, facilitators or obstructors. In the agenda-setting phase of this bill, they acted as facilitators. They were not the first groups to place housing on the agenda, but they also did not obstruct it. Instead, they facilitated the agenda-setting process by providing information and policy alternatives in response to congressional activity, adapting their own agendas to the attitudes and behavior of members of Congress.[19]

POLICY FORMULATION

In March 1989, two housing bills were introduced in Congress. The House and Senate bills each took a different approach to housing policy, and the administration had a third perspective. In the following year and a half, the three alternatives were debated by interest groups, including the government groups. The state and local groups used the eight tactics identified by Haider to lobby for housing legislation:

1. Use access and get the matter on the agenda
2. Build coalitions—Form alliances
3. Nourish your allies
4. Exploit cleavages
5. Gear strategies to the legislative climate
6. Count heads and money
7. Research—Counterresearch
8. Grass roots efforts

The state and local groups concentrated on the first, sixth and seventh tactics. They made sure that their policy alternatives were part of the congressional agenda by testifying at hearings and releasing information on the housing problem. They counted money more than heads: the state and local groups were most concerned with the split of money for the HOP program and appropriations for the National Affordable Housing Act. They also concentrated on research: releasing reports with statistics on housing problems and proposed policies.

Splitting over Funding

The biggest issue for state and local groups was the funding split for the HOP program in the Senate bill. Originally, the bill formula-funded 80% of HOP money, dividing it 50-50 between states and localities. NGA and NCSL were satisfied with the split. Although the groups would have preferred more money going to the states, they were willing to accept 50%. Local governments were strongly opposed to the split. They wanted the money to be divided the same way the Community Development Block Grant is, with 70% going to local government, 30% to state government. The state and local groups were thus pitted against one another, and the result was a compromise 60-40 (local-state) split that made it difficult to determine who actually won.

The local groups began lobbying for a greater percentage of funds even before the housing bill was introduced. At the Senate subcommittee hearings on the Rouse-Maxwell report, the NLC, USCM and NACO all testified in favor of a 70-30 funding split. The groups, especially the League, "never let up" pressure on the issue, according to one respondent. In the words of a congressional staffer, it was "the biggest issue for the cities and they fought it tooth and nail right down to the end." The NGA was fighting on the other side. Both groups made their position known through testimony and direct contact with legislators and their staffs. The NCSL testified in favor of a 50-50 split, but did not lobby strongly beyond that testimony. Respondents indicated that the NLC was the most vocal of the groups on either side, and that NLC, USCM and NACO banded together in a coalition on the issue.

Both congressional and association staff gave credit to the local groups for changing the funding split, but there was some disagreement as to whether the 60-40 split was a win or a loss. One local group staffer said it was "our biggest win." Another called it a loss, because the local governments did not get the 70% that they wanted. At least one congressional staffer called the governors the winners, because the states ended up with more money than the local governments wanted them to have. The funding split was similar to a divisive issue in the late 1960s, whether the Crime Control and Safe Streets Act of 1968 would be funded by block grants distributed by states, or project grants to local communities.[20] In 1968 the governors won. In 1990 the localities were more successful.

The issue of the funding split was very important to the local groups as well as the NGA, but some congressional actors felt that the groups were focusing on it to the exclusion of more substantive issues and to the detriment of consensus building. One congressional respondent was critical of the groups' activities with regard to the split, saying, "Here you had a major restructuring of housing policy and the need to build a strong solid coalition of support, but the groups were fighting over scraps." Of course, the groups did not perceive the money as "scraps," and this points to a significant difference between the priorities of congressional actors and government groups. Congress is organized into committees based on substantive issues, so it focuses on "functional" rather than "spatial" or geographic issues. Government groups, on the other hand, are more interested in geographic issues. So the groups focused on which level of government would get a larger piece of the funding pie, while Congress (and other interest groups) were more interested in development of specific programs. In general, urban government interests most often have to do with the allocation of resources.[21]

The local interest groups in the 1960s and 1970s were the beneficiaries of direct federal-city programs. Although that began to change in the 1980s, the cities reacted to the funding issue by asserting the localities themselves as an interest. "Urban intergovernmental lobbying has entrenched the practice of the 'third' level of government (cities) pressuring the 'first' level (federal) and bypassing the 'second' level (states)."[22] The local groups employed several of the tactics that Haider described. They used their access to get the matter on the agenda from the beginning of the process. NLC, NACO and USCM formed an alliance to put pressure on members of Congress to "count money" to local governments' satisfaction. No other interest groups became significantly involved in the debate over funding.

Alphabet Soup: HOP, HOME and HOPE

The Block Grant Approach

A second important issue for the groups was the general approach of using a block grant for the new housing programs. The Senate bill was based on the Housing Opportunity Program (HOP), a block grant that was renamed HOME Investment Partnerships in conference, and that provided for new construction of public housing, which the administration opposed. The state and local groups favored HOP over the administration's Homeownership Opportunities for People Everywhere (HOPE) program. All of the groups testified in favor of HOP in the hearing process, and all but NCSL testified in opposition to the HOPE program. Their position on HOP was due to obvious reasons. Regardless of the funding split between states and localities, a new housing block grant would mean more money to subnational governments with fewer strings attached. Here was a case where the spatial concerns of the government groups were addressed in congressional legislation. Government interest group policy is usually in favor of increasing general purpose funding and decreasing the number of categorical grants.[23]

While all of the respondents mentioned the HOP (HOME) program as something in which the government groups were interested (one said, "HOME was the primary emphasis for the state and locals"), neither congressional nor association staff gave them full credit for the inclusion of a block grant in the housing bill. While the groups lobbied for the flexibility of a block grant approach, there were other more pressing reasons to include HOP (HOME) in the final legislation. The Democrats in Congress compromised with the administration by agreeing to include Kemp's HOPE program in exchange for the HOME block grant, which was slightly modified to avoid a presidential veto.

The HOME program, in that it is more flexible than most state-federal programs, is a "win" for the state and local groups. "The biggest winners may be state and local governments. Assuming that appropriators follow the authorizers' lead next year, federal housing policy is in for a turnaround. Using a block grant, state and local governments will have more to say when putting together housing programs with federal dollars."[24]

However, a broad coalition of other interest groups was more involved in the HOP program deliberations. The Council of Large Public Housing Authorities (CLPHA), the National Association of Housing Redevelopment Officials (NAHRO),[25] the Enterprise Foundation, the Local Initiatives Support Corporation (LISC), the National Community Development Association (NCDA) and the Low-Income Housing Coalition were part of a loose umbrella coalition that lobbied for the HOME program. A congressional staffer concluded that "the mere fact that a bill passed was because it had a broad-based appeal, there was momentum, there was an umbrella coalition."

The government groups' primary approach with regard to the use of the HOME block grant was to gear their strategy to the legislative climate. Since it appeared that the HOME program was necessary for the Democrats to approve a bill, and since there was a coalition supporting the HOME program, the state and local groups limited their activities to getting their voices on record through testimony and limited contact with congressional staff. There was no sense wasting resources on an issue that was bound to be resolved favorably anyway. Even in the 1960s, "the mayors tended to depend upon their housing experts, the National Association of Housing and Redevelopment Officials, for shaping much of their housing policy."[26]

The Issues of Matching Grants and New Construction

Although the state and local groups were in favor of a block grant approach in general, there were specifics of the HOP program to which they objected. The government groups were in favor of the use of grants for new construction of low-income housing (as were other interest groups); the administration was opposed to federal funding of new construction. In order to get a bill that would not be vetoed by the President, the Senate bill included a matching requirement that would vary according to funding use: states and localities would match 25% of funds used for rental assistance, 33% of funds used for rehabilitation and 50% of funds used for new construction. The state and local groups felt this was too restrictive, and favored the House Democrats' approach of requiring an across-the-board 25% match. Despite lobbying by the state and local groups, the Senate version was included in the final bill. The compromise was necessary to get the bill signed by the President, who opposed new construction and favored having states pay more of the costs for it. An association staffer said that the groups lost by "not convincing the administration" of the need for a more flexible match. The compromise meant that not only would the state and local governments need to spend more money, but they would be penalized for spending money on the activity they felt was most important, new construction. Several respondents claimed that the compromise was necessary to get the President's signature.

Interestingly, the state and local governments were not opposed to a match in general. The NGA and USCM testified at the beginning of the process that they would be willing to provide money for a new housing bill. On the other hand, they were also strongly in favor of provisions for new construction. The government groups used their access effectively in Congress, but not in the administration. The state and local groups were on the same side of the issue, but did not really develop an alliance. They nourished their allies, and geared their strategies to the legislative climate, by offering to contribute funding to housing. Unfortunately for them, the President and his administration (including HUD Secretary Jack Kemp) were adamantly opposed to new construction, and it is unclear whether stronger lobbying of the administration on the part of the government groups would have resulted in a more favorable match.

The D'Amato/Dodd Mega-Block Grant: The National League of Cities Creates Trouble

An alternative proposal submitted by Senators D'Amato and Dodd in April 1990 (S. 2504, the Grant Action Program [GAP]), would have consolidated nine existing housing programs, including all public housing and other small categorical programs, into a block grant. Rather than creating new programs, it would give state and local governments flexibility in determining how best to spend existing housing funds. One respondent called the proposal a "mega-HOME." State and local governments, which generally react favorably to block grants, were placed in a difficult predicament. GAP would address their spatial concerns, but if the groups supported it, they would be turning their backs on three years of work by housing advocates in Congress. The GAP program would have eliminated HOP, the Democrats' pet proposal.

Most government groups, adhering to Haider's strategy of nourishing allies, were reluctant to take a stand on the legislation. Although the groups would have liked to support the block grant, they did not want to alienate congressional supporters of HOP. There were two exceptions. The U.S. Conference of Mayors, whose membership tends to be more Democratic, was strongly opposed to the proposal (as were housing advocacy groups). The National League of Cities, which represents smaller cities, and thus has more conservative members, came out in favor of the proposal. They saw cleavages in Congress, and chose to use Haider's strategy of exploiting them. Some congressional staffers felt that the League was actually involved in developing the proposal. But the League has traditionally had better relationships with the Republican party, and is not as "urban-oriented" as the USCM.[27]

It is not unusual for the Conference and the League to take opposite positions on policy. It was, however, unusual for the League to take a stand on a controversial issue. Although its membership is more Republican and more conservative than the Conference's, there are liberal-conservative cleavages within the NLC; its members are much less homogeneous than the USCM's. Since it is difficult to build consensus among the members, the organization generally avoids controversial issues.[28] In this case, the cities had much to gain from the program. They would receive a great deal of money with very few strings attached. But congressional respondents felt the proposal generated a lot of bitterness. Those in Congress who favored the HOP program felt that it would create the possibility for increased funding, while the GAP program would guarantee funding, although at lower levels. The debate was similar to the controversy in child care over the use of Title XX (guaranteed money) or a new program (with the possibility for greatly increased funding.) Some of the congressional respondents felt that the NLC was more or less going behind the backs of the Congressional Democrats with whom they had been working. One respondent said that there was a perception that the NLC had "torpedoed" the HOME legislation. Another said that the NLC was working with D'Amato without telling the other congressional actors.

The Democratic members of Congress "wanted a strong statement of opposition" to the D'Amato/Dodd block grant, but it was "difficult to get a governor to give a personal commitment," according to a congressional respondent. Congressional staff called the NGA to get letters of support from governors, but no governor was willing to oppose the D'Amato/Dodd block grant publicly. A congressional staffer said, "When we needed them, we couldn't get them." However, the NGA did not endorse the GAP block grant, choosing to remain silent on an issue that presented the groups with a difficult choice. And there was no lead governor to speak out in opposition to the block grant.

A compromise was eventually reached in conference committee, leaving most public housing intact, but killing ten small programs worth about $551 million, which would be shifted to HOP, rather than consolidating the large housing programs in a single block grant. The failure of the D'Amato/Dodd block grant was to be expected, because "efforts to change the grant system tend uniformly to meet opposition to the extent that they involve elimination or consolidation of grants . . ."[29]

Other Issues

The Community Development Block Grant

The Community Development Block Grant (CDBG), a perennial favorite of state and local governments, was tied to the National Affordable Housing Act. The grant, which gives flexible funding to local and state governments (under a 70-30 split), was up for reauthorization. State and local groups wanted to make certain the CDBG was funded at current levels, that HUD did not put new restrictions on it, and that Section 108 loan guarantees were expanded. They were successful in getting funding for the block grant and expanding community development loan guarantees to include guarantees for construction of low and moderate-income housing for home ownership, and were partially successful in keeping the block grant flexible, although the low and moderate-income targeting requirement was increased form 60% to 70%.

Preservation

The state and local groups did not really take a stand on preservation of low-income housing units. The owners of the units and non-profit advocacy groups fought over the issue, eventually reaching a compromise in which owners would be compensated at fair market values in exchange for preserving their housing developments for low-income tenants. If the community had high vacancy rates, the owners could pay off their loans and convert the housing to whatever use they wanted.

Reform of the FHA Fund

Another issue that was controversial in the bill, but in which state and local groups did not play a part, was the reform of the FHA fund, which was heading toward insolvency. The groups that were involved were the National Association of Home Builders, the National Association of Realtors and the Mortgage Bankers' Association. The compromise involved requiring first-time buyers to pay additional upfront costs and annual insurance fees. A respondent noted that the realtors' groups withdrew their support for the entire bill because of the compromise.

LEGITIMATION

The National Affordable Housing Act was signed by President Bush on November 28, 1990. According to respondents, the success of the bill was due to the ability of the Senate, House and administration to compromise. Each had its own version of housing legislation, and all three were merged into the bill, which included HOPE, HOME and Gonzalez's National Housing Trust Fund. According to a congressional respondent, the "smart money" in 1990 was betting that a housing bill could not pass, that it would be too difficult to achieve consensus among these three entities. The fact that a bill was passed at all was considered a win by almost everyone involved.

Most of the compromising was within the federal government. However, interest groups played some role in the process. Housing advocates as well as state and local groups helped keep housing on the agenda, and various groups played roles in compromising on issues. Once the bill was passed, the state and local groups kept up their lobbying to make sure that it was fully funded in the appropriations process. Several respondents mentioned that the groups were much more active in appropriations than in authorizations. They were successful. Although the initial bill funded HOME at $3 billion for fiscal year 1991, the House funded HOME at only $500 million, the Senate at $2 billion. The groups got $1.5 billion (closer to the Senate figure than to the House figure) as a result of intense lobbying. There was a "reluctance to fund HOME on the House side, because they weren't the authors." The groups lobbied persistently, using direct member contact and grassroots support (NACO started a "Bring America HOME" postcard campaign among its members). They were able to get $1.5 billion for fiscal 1992. Respondents almost universally credited the state and local groups with getting increased funding for the HOME program. Many suggested that this was the government groups' (especially the local groups') greatest success.

Respondent Perception of Impact

Congressional and association staff were asked in the interviews to rate the impact of various interest groups on the legislation. First, respondents were asked which groups they felt were most influential in the passage of the legislation. They were asked to rate the impact of those groups (10 being the highest rating, one the lowest). Next, they were asked to rate any of the five state and local groups that were not mentioned in their previous answers. A summary of the results is included in Table 4.1. Other than state and local groups, only those groups mentioned by at least two respondents are listed. The state and local groups did not make it into the top four. None of the government groups achieved as high a rating as did the NGA on child care (7.4). The NCSL received the lowest rating; the local groups received the highest among the government groups. The Enterprise Foundation (which was part of the initial task force, but which lobbied separately from it), NAHRO, LISC and NCDA received higher rankings than did the government groups. These groups were lobbying on some of the more high profile issues, such as

Table 4.1 Ratings of Interest Group Impact on Housing Legislation

Enterprise Foundation	8.0
NAHRO	8.0
LISC	7.7
NCDA	7.2
USCM	6.8
CLPHA	6.5
NLC	6.5
NACO	5.1
NGA	5.0
NCSL	1.3

Scores are averages of respondents' ratings of interest group impact. "10" means very high impact; "1" very low impact.

preservation and FHA, and acted in a coalition. The government groups expended their energies on an issue that congressional respondents did not perceive as very important, the funding split, and they did not act in concert. Respondents mentioned the government groups as being significantly involved, and many said that it was necessary to get their support in order for a bill to pass. However, respondents credit other groups with having a more significant impact on the overall bill.

However, the government groups did appear to have some impact on the bill, with the local groups (especially NLC and USCM) having a fairly substantial effect. The two issues in which respondents said the groups had a significant impact were funding issues: the state-local split and full-funding of the authorizing legislation. These and the matching issue were their most important concerns. The state-local split was resolved in favor of the local governments, and the local governments were more significantly involved in lobbying for funding.

Several respondents had difficulty answering the question and did not want to be pressed to state a specific number for any one group. Most of those who did not answer the question specifically discussed the importance of several groups working together, noting that, in the words of one respondent, it would be difficult "to single out" the effects of any one group. Some of those who did not answer the question were association staff, which may indicate that they did not want to give their own groups a low rating. However, some of those who did not answer were congressional respondents, who have fewer personal reasons for not wanting to rate the groups. It may be simply that the combination of interest groups was more important than any one actor.

A congressional staffer offered what may be an alternative explanation. According to him, the bill was unusual because Congress was "proactive" in putting together legislation, rather than waiting for the administration or interest groups to act. From the time Cranston was appointed to the chair of the Housing subcommittee in the Senate in 1987, he pushed for housing legislation. It was at his suggestion that the task force was created, he requested input on the task force's recommendations and he introduced the bill that eventually became the National Affordable Housing Act. In contrast, the child care bill, although it had strong advocates in Congress, was really the product of the ABC coalition, which acted as the policy entrepreneur. No outside group acted in such a way for the housing legislation; all of the groups essentially reacted to congressional actors' proposals. Perhaps because the Reagan administration had placed a low priority on housing, the interest groups were not willing to expend resources in an area in which they were uncertain of success. Even when George Bush became President and appointed an activist HUD secretary, the groups were not inclined to lobby for housing. According to a congressional respondent, most actors in the housing arena felt that a housing bill would not pass in 1990.

It may be that those respondents who did not wish to answer the question were reflecting the view that the impetus for the legislation came from within Congress rather than without, and those who did answer were referring to specific legislative provisions to which the groups reacted and on which they eventually had an impact. The interest groups may not have been the driving force for the legislation the way the ABC Alliance was for child care, but they did have an impact.

Group Positions on Specific Provisions

Table 4.2 lists some major provisions of the legislation as passed, and whether the state and local groups were in favor of that particular provision, opposed, or did not have a strong lobbying position. The other interest groups are not included in the table because they were concerned with different provisions. Counting partial wins as wins, the NGA had two wins, three losses; NCSL, two wins, two losses; and NLC, USCM and NACO, four wins, two losses. The results of the local groups are not surprising, but NCSL, which was given a rating of 1.3 on impact, had a better ratio of wins to loses than NGA, which was rated 5 on impact. This can be explained by the fact that Table 4.2 does not take the level of lobbying effort into consideration. While NCSL had specific positions on the legislation, by all accounts the group did not lobby

Table 4.2 State and Local Government Groups' Positions on
Legislative Provisions (Housing)

	NGA	NCSL	NLC	USCM	NACO
HOME Block Grants	+	+	+	+	+
CDBG	+	+	+	+	+
Matching	-	-	-	-	-
Funding Split	-	-	+	+	+
HOPE	-	0	-	-	-
Funding Level	0	0	+	+	+

+   Provision is consistent with stated group policy
-   Provision is in opposition to stated group policy
0   Group did not take a strong lobbying position on this provision
+/- Provision is partially consistent with stated group policy on this provision

heavily. On the other hand, the local groups lobbied more extensively on the housing legislation. They received higher ratings than the state groups, and their ratio of wins to losses was higher. It appears that their lobbying efforts paid off. Although they were not successful on every issue, they were successful on the funding split, in which they opposed the state groups.

CONCLUSIONS

The state and local interest groups used all of the tactics identified by Haider. They used their access to ensure that housing was on the agenda. All of the groups participated to some degree in the agenda-setting phase by presenting research at hearings or in published reports about the housing problems. They formed coalitions over specific issues, with the local groups bonding together on the funding split, and all of the groups lobbying together for the use of a block grant approach. Most of the groups nourished their allies by not taking a stand on the D'Amato/Dodd block grant, although the NLC exploited cleavages in a futile attempt to get a more flexible block grant. They geared strategies to the legislative climate by not expending excess energy on proposals that would have passed anyway, and they counted money by lobbying on the funding split and the funding level. NACO employed grassroots efforts to get its members to lobby to "Bring America HOME," in a successful effort to increase appropriated funds for the act.

The National Affordable Housing Act falls into Haider's third category of legislation: zero-sum, intergroup conflict legislation, in which benefits are expected to flow from one level of government to the other. The issue that was most important to the groups was the split of funding, and either group's win would mean the other group's loss. In this case, the local governments won. The fact that the groups were pitted against each other over this issue meant that they also did not form a significant coalition for other legislative issues. When the groups act separately from one another, then their strength as intergovernmental actors is reduced.

NOTES

1. Also known as the Rouse-Maxwell Commission, so-named after the chair and vice chair, James Rouse from the Enterprise Foundation and David Maxwell from Fannie Mae.

2. The act authorized $443 million for fiscal 1987 and $616 million for fiscal 1988 to set up emergency shelters and food programs, and make medical care and job training available for the homeless, in addition to setting aside funds for homeless persons with special problems, such as mental illness.

3. Farkas, *Urban Lobbying*, pp. 21–22.

4. Reported in "Billions in U.S. Aid Urged for Low-Income Homes," *New York Times*, March 29, 1988, sec. B, p. 20.

5. U.S. Congress, Senate, Committee on Banking, Housing and Urban Affairs, *The National Affordable Housing Act. Hearings before the Subcommittee on Housing and Urban Affairs.* 100th Cong., 2nd sess., 1988.

6. Gwen Ifill, "City Leaders Decry Lack of Affordable Housing," *Washington Post*, January 13, 1989, sec. A, p. 7.

7. Ann Mariano, "Who Will Get Government Housing Aid?" *Washington Post*, January 28, 1989, sec. F, pp. 1, 2.

8. Robin Toner, "Senate Gets Housing Measure Aimed at Keeping Costs Low," *New York Times*, March 16, 1989, sec. A.

9. Phil Kuntz, "Expiring Federal Subsidies Raise a Policy Dilemma," *Congressional Quarterly Weekly Report*, May 6, 1989, pp. 1041–1042.

10. Ibid, p. 1042.

11. Phil Kuntz and Joan Biskupic, "New Investigations Launched as HUD Scandal Widens," *Congressional Quarterly Weekly Report*, June 17, 1989, p. 1477.

12. Democrats in Congress wanted to tie new housing programs to HUD reform legislation, in the hope that it would speed housing expansion through Congress. Eventually, HUD reform was separated from affordable housing

legislation, but only after the Bush administration developed its own proposal for affordable housing.

13. U.S. Congress, Senate, Committee on Banking, Housing and Urban Affairs, *The National Affordable Housing Act, Hearings before the Subcommittee on Housing and Urban Affairs*, 100th Cong., 2nd sess., 1988, pp. 174–175. Testimony of Raymond G. Scheppach, executive director, National Governors' Association.

14. Ibid., Testimony of Jessie Rattley, mayor of Newport News, Virginia.

15. Ibid., Testimony of Michael Hightower, county commissioner, Fulton County, Georgia.

16. Richard L. Berke, "Dukakis Says He Would Commit $3 Billion to Build New Housing," *New York Times*, June 29, 1988, p. 21.

17. Ann Mariano, "New Congress, Bush to Face Housing Crisis," *Washington Post*, January 14, 1989, sec. E, pp. 1, 8.

18. Clifford D. May, "Kemp Puts Focus on Urban Change," *New York Times*, June 20, 1989.

19. Haider, *When Governments Come to Washington*, p. 213.

20. Ibid., pp. 182–192.

21. Farkas, *Urban Lobbying*, p. 26.

22. Ibid., p. 235.

23. Haider, *When Governments Come to Washington*, p. 213.

24. Jill Zuckman, "Conferees' Authorization Bill Marks Turnabout in Policy," *Congressional Quarterly Weekly Report*, October 20, 1990, p. 3514.

25. Haider defines this as a "public official organization" (PORG) government interest group.

26. Haider, *When Governments Come to Washington*, p. 227.

27. Farkas, *Urban Lobbying*, p. 164.

28. Haider, *When Governments Come to Washington*, p. 37.

29. Ibid, p. 87.

Chapter 5

The Governors Get Their Way: Welfare Reform

In his January 1986 State of the Union address, President Ronald Reagan suggested reforming the welfare system. Almost three years later, in October 1988, he signed the Family Support Act into law. In those three years, the National Governors' Association helped Democrats and Republicans in Congress forge compromises with each other and with administration officials. Although many actors were involved in welfare reform consideration, the key factor may have been what Senator Moynihan called "syzygy," in astronomy, a rare alignment of the earth, moon and sun, or in this case, a new consensus among liberals and conservatives that welfare recipients should both be required to be involved in some type of employment activity and be given some level of supportive services (such as child care) to assist in their participation in work and training programs.[1] The legislation included an expansion of benefits (making welfare benefits mandatory for two-parent families in which the primary wage earner is unemployed), beefed-up child support enforcement provisions, a program to encourage welfare recipients to engage in work or training activities (Job Opportunities and Basic Skills or JOBS), and expanded support services to those who did. Although the Family Support Act did not go as far as either liberals or conservatives wanted (it did not create a minimum national benefit or require recipients to work for their benefits), it was the most significant restructuring of the Aid to Families with Dependent Children (AFDC) program since its inception in 1935.

In contrast to both child care and housing legislation, one government group was actively involved throughout the agenda-setting phase as well as during consideration in Congress. The National Governors' Association played a role similar to that of the ABC coalition and the Affordable Housing Task Force. The group developed a welfare policy proposal that became the basis for legislation introduced in Congress. Like the task force's housing proposal, the

NGA welfare reform proposal was not introduced verbatim but became the focal point for discussion of the issue. Like the ABC coalition, the NGA was a vocal and active advocate for its proposal not only at the agenda-setting phase but throughout the legislation's consideration. Almost all respondents, as well as media reports, credit the NGA with putting welfare reform on the agenda and ensuring its passage. Although others gave credit to Senator Moynihan, some congressional respondents said that his role was overstated. One person said, "We passed the bill in spite of Moynihan, not because of him." The NGA as a "policy entrepreneur" was different from the ABC coalition and the housing task force: it was a single interest group, rather than an umbrella organization encompassing several interest groups. While the coalition represented advocacy groups and the task force was made up of research organizations, the NGA was a group of government officials with firsthand experience in implementing and developing welfare proposals. In this case, the NGA's elected official status heightened its influence in the policymaking process, and, in a role that is somewhat unusual for a government group, the NGA acted as an initiator as well as a facilitator for the legislation.[2]

The NGA was instrumental in placing and keeping welfare reform on the policy agenda, but it was not successful in all of its goals. In particular, the governors had been opposed to mandatory work requirements and minimum participation rates for the number of welfare recipients in employment or training activities, both of which were included in the final bill. Nevertheless, almost all actors involved considered the NGA to have had a significant impact on the passage of the legislation. In this issue area, local groups, as well as the National Conference of State Legislatures, played a relatively minor role. The National Association of Counties was somewhat more active than the other two local groups: welfare programs are administered at the county, not city, level.

AGENDA-SETTING

Background

The modern welfare system in the United States was begun in 1935 with the passage of the Social Security Act. Within that act was the Aid to Dependent Children (ADC) program, which was designed to help a surviving family when its primary wage earner died or was unable to work. Authors of the legislation envisioned the program assisting families where the death or incapacitation of the father might leave the mother with no means of supporting her family. ADC benefits went only to the children in such families. In 1950, Congress expanded ADC to include the children's mothers as well, renaming the program Aid to Families with Dependent Children (AFDC). In 1961, the program was expanded, at state option, to include two-parent families where the main wage earner was unemployed, enlarging the program to include fathers as well.

By the 1960s, there was a general perception that the AFDC program was not solving the root problems of poverty. Liberals believed that benefits were insufficient, while conservatives felt that welfare recipients were being discouraged from working. Proposals in Congress and the White House attempted to address these concerns. First Congress established the Work Incentive Program (WIN) in 1967, which required states to make work or training programs available to adult welfare recipients, and allowed states to develop federally funded demonstration programs that encouraged work. However, the feeling that AFDC was inadequate persisted, and in 1969 President Richard Nixon proposed a complete overhaul. His Family Assistance Program (FAP), the most liberal presidential welfare reform proposal before or since, would have given a guaranteed minimum income to families with children. FAP eventually died in conference in 1972.[3] Five years later, President Jimmy Carter proposed his own version of welfare reform, Program for Better Jobs and Income. The program would have combined AFDC, Food Stamps and the Supplemental Security Income (SSI) program (cash assistance for the elderly and disabled) into a single cash grant. The proposal never passed Congress.[4]

After Reagan was elected to office on an anti-big government campaign, he persuaded Congress to make cuts in the welfare program. The Omnibus Budget and Reconciliation Act (OBRA) of 1981 restricted AFDC eligibility and expanded work requirements. The changes resulted in eliminating an estimated 442,000 families from AFDC caseloads. The following year, Reagan proposed a "turnback" program in which states would take over AFDC in return for the federal government assuming the full cost of Medicaid and other medical programs. The proposal got nowhere in Congress, and state and local officials objected vehemently to it.[5] Throughout the 1960s, 1970s and 1980s, then, the government repeatedly attempted to reform the welfare system, but succeeded only in implementing minor changes.

The Problem Stream

In 1987, welfare reform again came to the top of the congressional agenda. As in child care and housing legislation, there was no "focusing event" that placed welfare reform on the agenda. Welfare reform seems to be a cyclical event. According to poverty scholar Leslie Lenkowsky, "every 25 years or so, we rediscover poverty . . . When the economy goes well, we begin to think about the poor. Every generation begins to feel guilty."[6] In welfare reform, feedback was the most important factor in the problem stream, while the child care and housing problem streams were characterized primarily by systematic indicators. Studies of the implementation of AFDC and WIN at the state level helped to identify problems in the welfare system. WIN demonstration programs created an opportunity for firsthand evaluation of work-welfare programs. Research from the WIN demonstrations was used both to identify the problem and develop possible solutions.

The nature of the welfare debate was framed in 1984 with publication of Charles Murray's *Losing Ground*, which brought the issue of work to the forefront. Murray claimed that not only was the welfare system inadequate to address the poverty problem, it actually was a *source* of the problem. According to Murray, social welfare policies in the United States had a net effect of increasing the poverty rate between 1950 and 1980, and these programs actually created a dependency on welfare.[7] Although many scholars disagreed with the factual basis of Murray's thesis,[8] his arguments were cited by conservatives as evidence that Great Society Programs in general and AFDC in particular were not accomplishing their intended goals. Conservatives had argued for years that the problem with welfare was that recipients were rewarded for not working; however, Murray's thesis went a step further and said that AFDC was encouraging dependency and long-term poverty. Eventually, both liberals and conservatives agreed that a reform of welfare must include emphasis on discouraging dependency by encouraging work.

While Murray's work was ideological in nature, subsequent studies attempted to measure more objectively the success of poverty programs. In February 1987, the American Enterprise Institute released a report by a group of twenty scholars it had brought together to study welfare. The group was called "The Working Seminar on Family and American Welfare Policy" and was made up of both liberals (including Alice Rivlin) and conservatives (including Charles Murray and Leslie Lenkowsky). Their report said that the welfare system is inadequate to discourage dependency among its recipients. According to the report, half of children born to mothers receiving AFDC are born out of wedlock, and only 9% of mothers receiving welfare worked for forty or more weeks in 1983, compared to 40% of non-poor mothers.[9]

The governors' role in agenda-setting was much more evident in the policy stream; however, governors were involved in the problem stream. For example, Governor Mario Cuomo of New York and Governor Bruce Babbitt of Arizona commissioned task forces to study welfare policy. Cuomo's Task Force on Poverty and Welfare released a report in 1986, which indicated that the problem with welfare was the lack of incentives for clients to work, and put forth the notion that welfare programs should be a contractual relationship between the government and the recipients.[10] Michael Castle, Governor of Delaware, testified on behalf of the NGA at Senate subcommittee hearings in 1987, where he suggested policy proposals and presented poverty statistics: about eight million working Americans do not earn enough to pay their living expenses, while twelve million Americans are on welfare. About six million of those on welfare are "hard-core" unemployed.[11]

Other systematic indicators demonstrated that welfare and poverty were problems. As in the child care debate, statistics on the influx of women into the workforce throughout the 1970s and 1980s added to the problem stream. Elected officials in the past had been reluctant to require mothers with young children to work. However, by 1986, half of the workforce was women. Thus, excluding welfare mothers from work requirements was perceived as unfair, because they were treated differently from other women in society.[12]

The most important contributions to the policy stream came from the states themselves. Several states had initiated work and training programs under the WIN demonstration program by the early 1980s. The Manpower Demonstration Research Corporation (MDRC) in 1982 began a five-year study of such initiatives in eight states: Arkansas, California, Illinois, Maine, Maryland, New Jersey, Virginia and West Virginia. In a report issued in 1987, MDRC summarized its findings for the eight states: work, education and training programs can decrease the number of long-term welfare recipients: 6% to 8% of recipients move off of welfare if they participate in work and training programs.[13] Although only a small proportion of clients was permanently eliminated from the welfare rolls, the general consensus was that the results were positive, that work and training were useful in decreasing dependency. The research was in fact part of the problem stream. Such work-welfare programs did not exist in every state, so to the extent the WIN demonstration programs were successful, they indicated inadequacies in states that had less innovative programs. If intensive education and training programs were the solution, then many states had a problem.

Individual state WIN initiatives were also the subject of research, and two in particular were heralded as model programs: Massachusetts's voluntary Employment and Training Choices program (ET Choices) and California's mandatory Greater Avenues for Independence (GAIN) program. The Massachusetts program was proclaimed in the mid-1980s to be highly successful in decreasing dependency and increasing wages, although later studies differed as to their assessments of its long-term effects.[14] States were developing their own ways of reforming welfare, and although these programs were funded by a federal match, their very existence indicated, at least to some scholars, that the AFDC program was in need of reform.

Of course, the fact that individual states were developing their own successful initiatives to encourage recipients to work might seem to indicate that the states were better able to develop individualized work and training programs than was the federal government. However, the WIN program, although popular with the states, was the victim of Reagan budget cuts throughout the 1980s. In addition, although states were using WIN funds to create new work programs, the Reagan budget cuts, combined with state budgetary constraints, meant a decline in welfare benefits.[15] Although Reagan was favorable toward allowing states to develop their own programs, he was uncomfortable with the amount of federal money devoted to WIN. In fact, Reagan would have preferred that states take over AFDC and related work programs completely. Members of Congress agreed in 1986 to eliminate funding for the WIN program entirely, hoping that it would be replaced by welfare reform legislation.[16] The expiration of WIN funding was a systematic indicator that there was an immediate problem in the welfare system. Coupled with the feedback from the WIN demonstration programs, the termination of WIN funding led to a perception of urgency in reforming the welfare system.

Most of the respondents claimed that the studies of the WIN demonstration programs and in particular, the MDRC study, had a significant impact on placement of welfare reform on the policy agenda. Many also mentioned that this type of reliance on research was unusual. According to one, "You'd like to think that public policy debates are fueled by that kind of information [the MDRC study], but that's very rare. They're fueled by political concerns, but often the substantive concerns fall by the wayside." Welfare reform was the exception. The MDRC studies, which were methodologically sound, and provided unequivocal data, were released just at the time Congress was beginning to consider welfare reform legislation. Moynihan's staff modeled the JOBS program after the findings in the MDRC study, which indicated that participants in WIN demonstration programs were more likely to get jobs at higher wages, that single mothers showed greater gains, and that benefits of the work programs would exceed the costs in the long run. MDRC, a non-partisan, non-profit organization, was recruited to testify on behalf of work-welfare programs before Congress.[17]

Studies of state initiatives also paved the way for the governors to enter the debate. Welfare reform provides an interesting contrast to child care and housing legislation. In housing, the federal government (Congress) started the process. In child care, advocacy groups initiated legislation. In welfare, state programs became the basis for discussion.

The Policy Stream

By 1987, the problem stream was clearly indicating a consensus that the welfare program was not functioning as intended, and that a reformed welfare system should discourage dependency and encourage work. As one respondent put it, "Republicans had discovered poverty and Democrats had discovered work." In response to the definitions of the problem, several policy suggestions were offered as solutions. First, in 1986, the House Democratic Caucus released a report by its Social Policy Task Force entitled "The Road to Independence," which recommended increasing aid to the working poor, and providing education and training programs for welfare recipients.[18] Later that same year the American Public Welfare Association (APWA), a group of state welfare administrators, called for replacing AFDC and food stamps with a new minimum family living standard. These proposals focused on the more liberal notion that welfare benefits should be increased, but they also agreed with the conservative idea that recipients should be encouraged to work.

Studies such as the ones by MDRC, Cuomo's task force and AEI's Working Seminar on Family Issues led to a consensus on the necessary ingredients for welfare reform: recipients should be provided with education and training opportunities to ease their transition to work; medical and child care benefits should be expanded to help both welfare recipients and the working poor; there should be some attempt to ensure that welfare benefits provide adequate living standards; and reform should focus on providing an environment for children that would discourage the generational cycle of poverty.[19]

As results from the studies were disseminated, congressional Democrats and Republicans, the White House, the National Governors' Association and the American Public Welfare Association developed policy proposals to address welfare reform. According to a congressional respondent, the process of developing proposals was "collaborative": interest groups (particularly the NGA and APWA) exchanged information and ideas with congressional staff. Then, the groups and Congress produced separate policy recommendations based on the collaborations. Several proposals were in the policy stream in 1987. The President had started the process in 1986, by calling for welfare reform in his State of the Union address and creating administration working groups to develop strategies for reforming welfare. In response, the Democratic Caucus's Social Policy Task Force released its report in mid-1986. The same year, APWA called for a new family living standard, which would require a state-by-state minimum benefit to replace AFDC cash assistance, Food Stamps and the Low Income Home Energy Assistance Program (LIHEAP). The APWA also later released a report that called for case management and a "contract" for welfare recipients.[20]

Senator Moynihan did not submit legislation until July 1987; however, in January of that year, he released his suggestions for welfare reform: require work or training for recipients and set minimum national benefits for welfare payments. He also began a series of hearings to discuss possibilities for reforming AFDC. At the hearings, he suggested enforcing child support payments from absent fathers, and noted that able-bodied mothers with children should be required to work. Representatives of all the state and local interest groups testified at these hearings. All of these groups were in favor of increasing child support enforcement, and requested flexibility for state and local governments. The NGA had the most specific proposals: a "family living standard," case management, and work requirements for mothers of children over three years old. The USCM testified against punitive workfare programs, instead insisting that employment and training programs must be voluntary. NLC requested that fiscal assistance be provided to local governments.[21]

In the meantime, the Reagan administration task force released its plan for reforming the welfare system in February 1987: the federal government would allow states the option of consolidating ninety-nine federal programs and developing their own welfare systems with waivers from the rules for AFDC. Reagan's proposal would not increase funding for welfare programs, but would instead create an optional block grant that gave states flexibility in determining how to spend federal funds. One respondent said the intent of the proposal was to "let a thousand flowers bloom," that is, let the states develop their own innovative proposals rather than having one federal program. The plan was so unpopular that even Reagan's own Departments of Education and Health and Human Services and the Veteran's Administration responded negatively, claiming that the Reagan policy would not provide legal protections for the poor and, by allowing states to lump non-welfare programs with food stamps and AFDC, would encourage spending that was not directed at the poor.[22] Interestingly, a similar Republican block grant proposal did not meet such vociferous objections in 1995.

By far the most influential policy proposal came out of the National Governors' Association annual meeting in February 1987. The NGA had set up a task force of six governors, headed by Clinton (D-Ark) and Castle (R-DE) in 1986 to develop a policy proposal in response to Reagan's call for welfare reform. The task force report was approved almost unanimously at the winter meeting.[23] The proposal suggested that the AFDC program be overhauled, changing its emphasis from income maintenance to education and training with a focus on case management. The governors also proposed that employment and training programs be made mandatory, that the program be an open-ended entitlement, that 85% of the initial funding come from the federal government (with the ultimate federal-state match being 75-25), and that states be given flexibility to distribute the funds. Their proposal suggested providing money for child care and extending Medicaid after the recipient left welfare. The NGA also suggested a gradual movement toward a state-by-state minimum standard, to be funded by savings from the expected reduction in the welfare rolls.[24]

The day the NGA proposal was passed, several governors presented it to a special meeting of the House Ways and Means Committee, a meeting that was called for the sole purpose of discussing NGA's suggestions. According to a respondent, "Almost everybody on the committee showed up. It was truly remarkable. They talked for several hours. It was a very informal kind of thing. The governors sat at the witness table but it was a . . . give and take exchange." The governors' proposal received a great deal of media attention, with one headline proclaiming "Governors Jump-Start Welfare Reform Drive." Once the NGA released its recommendations, Congress and the administration agreed to work with the governors to produce legislation. Reagan met with the governors on February 23 and he told them he supported their proposal for work and training, but would not agree to the proposed costs of the proposal, although Senator Pete Domenici (R-NM) had told the governors that he was prepared to spend "some money" on welfare reform. Moynihan and Harold Ford (D-TN, chair of the House Ways and Means Subcommittee on Public Assistance), agreed to develop a bill based on NGA's recommendations, and House Speaker Wright announced he would schedule welfare reform legislation in the spring. Even Clinton was surprised at the positive response the welfare issue received in Congress:

> If somebody told me five days ago that we'd get the president to agree to the basic outline and have Senator Moynihan and Congressman Ford ask us to participate in reviewing a common bill, and have the Speaker of the House say that we ought to do it right away, and have Senator Domenici say he thought it was worth funding even if you had to take money away from something else to do it, I wouldn't have believed it.[25]

Eventually two separate bills were introduced which reflected the governors suggestions: H.R. 1720 in the House, and S. 1511 in the Senate. "Promoted by the gubernatorial lobbying team of Arkansas Democrat Bill Clinton and Delaware Republican Michael N. Castle, the governors' plan ultimately became the basis for major welfare bills in both houses."[26] H.R. 1720, introduced by Ford in March 1987, created a National Education Training and Work (NETWork) program, which would be mandatory for welfare clients. The bill also established a minimum floor for benefits, made AFDC-UP mandatory,[27] and required states to increase efforts to collect child support. The bill would also require the federal government to pay 75% of the costs of the new program. Ford had vowed to work with the governors to develop legislation. According to one respondent, the "legislation was almost totally consistent with the governors' policy, [although] it was a little bit more expansive and contemplated spending a little bit more money." The Reagan administration was adamantly opposed to the bill: Office of Management and Budget (OMB) director James Miller called the bill a "travesty and a tragedy," while HHS secretary Otis Bowen wrote a letter to Rostenkowski in which he said the "bill would dramatically increase dependency at huge additional costs."[28] What the administration objected to most was the price tag of the bill, which was estimated to be about $5 billion over three to five years. (The estimates increased as the bill went through the House.) The program would have open-ended funding and would cover transportation and child care costs for recipients participating in work programs. The administration also remained vehemently opposed to an increase in benefits to clients, which it suggested would increase dependency.

Somewhat more acceptable to the administration was the Family Security Act, introduced by Moynihan in July 1987. Moynihan's bill included provisions for automatic withholding of child support payments from the absent parent's pay check, required states to increase efforts to establish paternity, provided child care to parents who participated in employment and training programs, extended child care and Medicaid for nine months after the recipient left welfare, made AFDC-UP mandatory, and created an employment and training program, Job Opportunities and Basic Skills (JOBS). Moynihan's bill did not have a minimum floor for benefits, and its cost was estimated at $2.3 billion over five years, significantly lower than the House bill's cost. Moynihan, who is himself considered an expert on welfare, gave the credit for his bill to the NGA: "In a sense, this is not my bill; it's the governors' bill."[29] In addition, he introduced the bill in the summer of 1987 to coincide with the governors' summer meeting. However, the bill was not totally consistent with what the governors wanted. It did not contain provisions for increasing benefits, and its requirements for states to increase efforts to establish paternity for AFDC children were overly prescriptive from the states' perspective.

Political Stream

The political stream for welfare reform was different from that for child care and housing legislation in that the presidential election had little to do with the reform effort. In contrast to the other issues, welfare reform had begun almost three years before Reagan was to leave office, and Reagan himself suggested the idea of reform. Whereas child care and housing advocates hoped to achieve reform after Reagan left office, welfare advocates were taken by surprise when Reagan announced his intent to reform the system in his 1986 State of the Union address. One respondent suggested that it was a mistake for a conservative president to propose overhauling welfare, suggesting that the "permanent lobby" (including groups like APWA, CDF, and other advocacy groups) for welfare would seize the opportunity to make the program more liberal.

Also in contrast to child care and housing, there was no perceived "crisis" in welfare. The increased number of women in the workforce led to a clamor for child care assistance for both middle and low-income families. The growing numbers of homeless people were a visible sign to the general public that there was a problem in housing. Although the Reagan administration had cut funding for AFDC as well as for housing programs, the effects were much less visible, and the middle class was less favorably inclined to helping welfare recipients than to addressing the homelessness problem. Even the studies that examined welfare reform in the states focused on the success of work programs rather than the failures of welfare initiatives. In addition, welfare recipients were a less potent constituency than were middle-income mothers with children or owners of low-income housing. Nonetheless, there were voices claiming a need for welfare reform. The system had remained virtually the same for almost thirty years, and the Reagan administration had cut benefits (adjusted for inflation) by as much as 33%.

The political stream for welfare was characterized by a sense of inevitability that reform would happen. Several respondents mentioned the word "syzygy" used by Moynihan in the initial hearings. Congressional and association staff felt that a rare alignment of forces caused the time to be ripe for welfare reform. One respondent said that it was "a very strange climate," that the late 1980s were a period of "more progressive, forward thinking," and that the feeling among people involved in the policy area was that it was "incumbent on us to do something." She characterized the period as a time of "new thinking" in welfare reform.

Welfare reform in the 1980s became both a liberal and a conservative issue. Publication of Charles Murray's book and the MDRC study gave conservatives something to be *for* in the welfare debate: instead of merely opposing liberal attempts to increase benefits, they began to advocate work programs to discourage dependency. When Reagan called for welfare reform, it legitimized conservative involvement in the issue, and created the possibility that reform might bring about changes consistent with the new conservative ideas. Liberals, on the other hand, were beginning to accept the idea of work programs, which were moving away from the more punitive "workfare" in which a client performs public work in exchange for her benefits and toward a "self-sufficiency" program, in which caseworkers assess clients' needs and develop strategies to get clients into the workforce permanently. Liberals still wanted to increase benefits and provide support services (such as child care, transportation and medical services), but they were willing to entertain the conservative ideas of work programs. What happened in the late 1980s, then, is that conservatives had developed a bargaining point. If liberals would agree to work requirements, conservatives would agree to supportive services. Suddenly, there was a quid pro quo in the welfare debate. And once there is a possibility for compromise, there is a possibility for legislation.

Of course, reforming welfare takes money, and the political environment included an economy that was still expanding, although there was a huge federal deficit. One respondent called welfare reform "one of the last great social change programs that we will see for some time." Several mentioned that such a program could not have passed in the current climate of fiscal constraint. Also, state governments experienced economic expansions in the 1980s, which led them to develop innovative work programs using WIN demonstration funds. The states were willing to put up money to reform the system on a national level, as long as the federal government would share the costs.

Perhaps the most important factor in the political stream was the number of activist governors who were willing not only to implement WIN demonstration programs in their states, but also to lobby aggressively for welfare reform at the national level. One congressional respondent who had been working on welfare issues since the early 1980s said that APWA and the NGA had not always been proponents of liberal welfare reform programs. She noted that in the 1970s the two groups were adamantly opposed to welfare reform and were, in fact, quite conservative on the issue. The "new thinking" that had affected national policymakers influenced these groups as well. And governors like Bill Clinton, Tom Kean, Michael Castle and John Sununu were pleased to act as spokespersons for the NGA's welfare reform drive, especially since it meant creating national names for themselves. "Much of the credit for the issue's sudden prominence was given to the National Governors' Association (NGA) which devoted virtually its entire annual midwinter meeting to the issue."[30]

Senator Moynihan too was part of the political stream. Moynihan, a colorful character described by one columnist as a "walking, talking exclamation point in a blue bow tie,"[31] had studied the welfare system for more than twenty years and was the author of Nixon's ill-fated FAP proposal, as well as books on welfare and the family. Early on, he announced his intention to develop a welfare reform proposal and to work with the governors to ensure that it met with their approval. When he assumed the chair of the Senate Subcommittee on Social Security and Family Policy, he used the position as a starting point from which to launch a campaign for welfare reform.

Several factors, then, were responsible for making the political stream favorable to welfare legislation, not the least of which was the willingness of the governors to lobby for reform. "Advocates of the legislation were buoyed by Reagan's vow in his 1986 State of the Union Address to make welfare reform a priority, by Moynihan's elevation to a subcommittee chairmanship from which he could exert a significant influence, and by an activist bipartisan group of governors eager for federal assistance for education and training programs."[32]

POLICY FORMULATION

The governors were as active in the policy formulation phase as they had been in the agenda-setting phase. Again, the other state and local groups played a relatively minor role, providing information where necessary, but in general keeping a much lower profile than the NGA. Other interest groups, particularly the APWA, also played a role in policy formulation, but none was as visible or as vocal as the National Governors' Association, which was present at nearly every debate over substantive issues. The governors used nearly all of the strategies identified by Haider: access, coalition-building, nourishing allies, exploiting cleavages, gearing strategies to the legislative climate, counting heads and money, research and grassroots efforts.

The governors' overriding concern in welfare legislation was to get a bill passed. While in child care their biggest issue was national standards, and in housing, the state-local funding split, the governors were less concerned with specific provisions in welfare reform. Although they had policy positions on several provisions, the governors were quite amenable to compromise. An association respondent asserted that the governors are more willing to compromise than other state and local groups. Because the governors' association is made up of both liberal and conservative members, all of whom are highly visible, the group does not generally take a stand unless it can achieve a consensus. And because the group is made up of prominent Republicans and Democrats, it has a greater ability to broker compromises in Congress.

The House Bill

Although there were two major welfare reform bills before Congress, they were introduced months apart (the House bill in February and the Senate bill in July 1987), giving the governors the ability to work compromises in each chamber individually. According to a congressional respondent, the NGA works one house at a time, brokering what deals it can, and then moving on to the other house, working on a new set of compromises. In the end, the governors will not support one bill over the other, preferring not to alienate members of either house. At the beginning of the welfare reform process, the House bill had the biggest price tag of the two and was the most comprehensive reform bill. The House bill was also more consistent with the governors' preferences.

The most remarkable activity of the NGA came as the House bill was being marked up by the House Ways and Means Committee. In an unprecedented move, Governor Clinton sat with the Ways and Means staff during the subcommittee mark-up and answered questions about how specific provisions of the bill would affect the states. According to a respondent, "Bill Clinton sat at the table with the committee. They ran all the amendments by him, they discussed what the governors would and would not find acceptable in terms of the amendments that were being offered. . . . the bill that was produced had tremendous gubernatorial support."

This is an example of the NGA using its access to its best advantage. Respondents were emphatic in stating that Clinton's presence at the mark-up was very unusual. No one could remember a time before or since when an outsider was so involved in the process. The NGA was considered an expert in the area of welfare reform by virtue of the state welfare programs that its members had created, so the group was accorded unprecedented access in the congressional policymaking process. "For a number of reasons the government groups find access to Congress, the White House and most executive agencies readily facilitated. . . . One of the principal resources that the government interest groups have is a certain legitimacy in standing."[33] In this case, that access was even greater than usual.

The governors' access was evident from the beginning of the process, when they presented their welfare proposal to a meeting of the House Ways and Means Committee called for that purpose. This too was unusual. The governors were treated differently in the House than interest groups usually are. Not only were they considered experts but also policymakers. Their status as elected government officials enhanced their ability to work with members of Congress.

Because the NGA was so involved in the process of formulating legislation, it is difficult to ascertain how much impact they had on particular provisions. In contrast to child care, where the governors took a strong stand on national standards and consistently fought to have their preferences addressed on the issue, the NGA did not stake out immovable positions on any provision in welfare reform, particularly as the bill was considered in the House. Their main concern was to have legislation passed. Compromises on particular provisions were ancillary to that concern. Nonetheless, there were two issues in the House bill that were the subject of some debate involving the governors: minimum benefits and the federal match.

Minimum Benefits

The House bill included a provision for minimum national benefits, a proposition that the governors endorsed in concept. Given their position on national standards in child care legislation, it seems unlikely that they would have supported a minimum benefit for welfare. Under the AFDC program, states set their own benefit levels and both the state and the federal government provide the money. Why would the governors want to set a national benefit, when they could do essentially the same thing by increasing benefits in their own states? The governors wanted to reform the welfare system, and they realized that inadequate benefits created a problem in many states. In addition, most states were, at the time, in periods of economic expansion, and were able to afford increases in benefits. They also hoped that employment and training provisions would decrease the number of recipients on the welfare rolls, which would offset the costs of the minimum benefits. One key difference between national standards in child care and a national minimum benefit in welfare reform is that child care is a traditional state function, while welfare has long been an integrated program.

The NGA's policy on a minimum benefit was the result of a compromise within the organization itself. The major focus of their welfare reform plan was on increasing work opportunities for recipients. While some of the more liberal Democratic governors wanted to include an increase in benefits, the more conservative governors would only agree to an increase if the policy statement stipulated that it would be paid for by AFDC savings realized from decreased caseloads. The position on minimum benefits also did not call for an immediate expansion but suggested, rather, "movement toward a cash assistance program which would ultimately be a state-specific family living standard developed according to a nationally-prescribed methodology and paid, as a minimum, at a nationally-prescribed percentage of that state's family living standard."[34] According to one association respondent, the governors are not as interested in long-term costs. Because they are generally in office for a shorter amount of time than elected officials from the other government groups, their concerns are more short-term.

The governors also knew that more liberal members in the House, in particular, Tom Downey (D-NY) who took over the chair of the Ways and Means Subcommittee on Public Assistance when Ford was forced to resign,[35] were in favor of minimum benefits. In addition, the governors were working with liberal interest groups such as APWA, who made minimum benefits a priority for welfare reform. Downey wanted not only to raise the minimum benefit (starting in 1993) but also to give financial incentives to states that increased their benefit levels before then. The governors "nourished their allies." Knowing that House Democrats were in favor of minimum benefits, the governors spoke out in support of such provisions. The government groups have always taken care of their allies on committees and subcommittees by providing them with research and information, or even drafting legislation and developing relationships with key constituent groups.[36] In this case, the NGA assisted its allies by helping draft legislation that would address their concerns. Also, they were willing to increase their own contributions as long as they knew the federal government would be providing more money, and giving the states flexibility on other issues such as work requirements.

The governors did not fully support the minimum benefit language in the Ways and Means Committee bill, because it required minimum benefits to begin in 1993, while the NGA had wanted the new minimum benefit to begin when savings from the work and training programs were realized. However, the NGA was willing to accept the provisions in order to pass the bill.

Although we have some problems with the way in which the subcommittee structured its proposed national minimum benefit level, we do believe that as Congress works with welfare reform this year, it should set in place a structure for an ultimate system. We believe H.R. 1720 is an excellent beginning.[37]

Federal Match

One reason why the governors accepted minimum benefits was because they were hoping for a favorable federal match for the new job training program.

Their policy statement called for the federal government to pay 85% of the costs the first year, decreasing to 75% of the costs by the fifth year. The governors also wanted the funding to be open-ended so that the federal government would match as much as the states were willing to spend, rather than having the entitlement capped at a certain amount. H.R. 1720 was fairly consistent with the governors' preferences: it started out with an open-ended 75-25 match for the NETWork program. However, the Reagan administration waiver proposal, Greater Opportunities Through Work (GROW) introduced in April 1987 by Rep. Hank Brown (R-CO), offered only a 50% match for states. Republicans were unhappy with the cost and the minimum benefits in the House Democratic bill, and in an effort to reduce costs, Ford lowered the federal government's share of funding to 60%. The governors would have preferred a more favorable match, but, realizing that a bill would have to be acceptable to Republicans, they accepted a 60-40 match, which was better than the 50-50 match proposed by the administration. In addition, they knew the issue could be taken up again in the Senate.

> Our policy does not prescribe any ideal match rate. . . . It seems to me that you have to have a match rate that is better than 50-50 if you want the poorest states, which often have the biggest problems, to develop quality programs. On the other hand, if you want to really serve everybody, it is better if you can avoid a cap, and that is why we wound up with 60-40 and no cap. . . . I would recommend that you stay with a match that is higher than 50-50, but if you have to come off the 75-25, to do away with the cap.[38]

The governors "counted money": they wanted a welfare reform bill to include significant money from the federal government. As an NGA representative said, "We believe the federal government is better at writing checks and the states are better at administering programs."[39]

House Passage of the Legislation

The Ways and Means Committee approved welfare reform in June 1987. NGA and APWA were pleased with the bill that came out of committee. The bill had a minimum benefit requirement starting in 1993, with financial incentives to states that increased their minimum benefits beforehand, mandated AFDC-UP, funded the NETWork program with a 60% federal match, allowed federal funding for day care services, and extended Medicaid coverage for nine months after a family left welfare due to increased earnings. Although the governors had given up some of what they wanted compared to their initial welfare reform policy, they strongly supported the bill that came out of the Ways and Means Committee, and pushed for passage in the House when it came up for a vote on December 16, 1987. Clinton published an editorial in the *Washington Post* the week before the House vote, comparing the administration's proposal to H.R. 1720, and claiming the Democrats' bill was better because it cost the states less money.[40]

Having worked extensively with the Ways and Means Subcommittee on Public Assistance, the governors, particularly Clinton, lobbied heavily for their bill. House Democrats initially tried to tie welfare reform to budget reconciliation, giving the legislation a ride on a "must-pass" bill. After congressional and administration Republicans objected to that idea, the Rules Committee scheduled the welfare bill separately. From mid-November until the House vote on December 18, the NGA worked extensively to ensure passage, focusing their efforts on Southern Democrats. The administration and House Republicans were opposed to H.R. 1720, and a Democrat, Thomas Carper (DE), had proposed a less expensive alternative that was more acceptable to Republicans, but included provisions to require a fixed percentage of recipients to participate in employment and training activities, a proposal anathema to the NGA. Afraid that Southern Democrats would support the proposal, House leadership delayed consideration several times. The governors' first step was to assist with the whip counts: NGA staff polled representatives and reported the numbers that would support the bill back to the majority whip.

At the same time, individual governors, particularly Clinton and Governor-elect Buddy Roemer (D-LA), worked on convincing Southern Democrats to vote for the bill. On December 3, Clinton attended a luncheon in the Capitol, where he spoke with several Southern Democrats who were inclined to vote against the bill. He also called and visited many of them in the final days before the vote. In the end, sixteen southerners were convinced to change their minds and vote in favor of H.R. 1720. Of course, House leadership was also putting pressure on the Southern Democrats, but the governors' role was crucial. "An intensive lobbying campaign by House leaders, one governor and one governor-elect split the so-called Boll Weevils [conservative Southern Democrats] and helped deliver the victory."[41]

In this case, the governors were quite successful at "counting heads" and gaining votes for the legislation. On crucial votes like this one, it is important for governors to lobby representatives from their states actively. According to a respondent, "they actively worked their delegations, worked the leadership and stayed constantly in touch and involved in what was going on." In addition to lobbying their own state delegations, Clinton and Roemer exploited their status as governors from southern states and broadened their lobbying efforts to include fence-sitting southerners from other states. Their efforts paid off. For example, Tim Valentine (D-NC), who voted for the bill after being heavily lobbied by Bill Clinton, said "I have been touched by the feelings of the governors more than anything else."[42] Haider also found the government groups were successful in delivering votes. The government groups often play a key role prior to important votes by both polling legislators to discover the fence sitters, and using strategic calls to garner the support of those who are undecided. Often, an undecided legislator may be influenced by last-minute contact from a governor or mayor.[43]

Senate Consideration

Although Moynihan's bill (S. 1511) was introduced in July 1987, it was not considered in the Senate until April of the following year. Because welfare reform had been such a partisan issue in the House, Senate leaders were leery of a contentious debate, and delayed action on the bill. Once the fight was over in the House, the governors turned their attention to the Senate bill. While the governors were at their annual meeting in Washington in February 1988, they met with Senators in an effort to hasten consideration of welfare reform. All of the governors attending the meeting signed a letter requesting that welfare reform be taken up soon, and four governors (Clinton, Castle, Sununu and Kean) met personally with Lloyd Bentsen, chair of the Senate Finance Committee, to deliver the letter. The four governors also met with President Reagan, who continued to push for his own waiver proposal. The purpose of the governors' activities was to keep welfare on the agenda. The state and local groups have always used personal visits to members of Congress, White House staff or executive branch officials to keep decision-makers focused on the need for a particular program. Visits or telephone calls serve to highlight the importance of immediate action and impress officials with the concerns of states and localities.[44]

The governors were not lobbying for one bill over another but concentrated on keeping the momentum going. Governor Castle said of the governors' activities, "Clearly, we're not endorsing any particular piece of legislation."[45] And even though Clinton had pressed for passage of the H.R. 1720, he wanted the Senate to pass a bill as soon as possible, so there would be room for compromise. "What I'd like to do is work out something: Get the Moynihan bill out of the Senate in some form or fashion, take it to conference and know what the real bottom line is, not all this sort of 'veto, veto' talk."[46]

The Senate bill was less expensive and expansive than the House version. Although both houses claimed their bill was in line with the outlines of the governors' policy on welfare reform, the House bill more accurately reflected their concerns. The NGA therefore lobbied for (or against) more specific provisions of the Senate bill. In particular, the association was concerned with "workfare" requirements and participation rates.

Workfare

The emerging consensus on welfare placed work at the center of any reform effort. But conservatives and liberals disagreed as to how to encourage recipients to work. Liberals wanted voluntary training and education programs to help clients develop skills that would keep them in the workforce. Conservatives wanted mandatory work requirements to ensure that people on welfare were earning their benefits, not just taking advantage of "the dole." The Reagan administration did not want a bill unless it included mandatory work requirements; liberal advocacy groups were adamantly opposed to such requirements. Senator Bob Dole (R-KS) ultimately came up with a compromise: include a provision mandating the AFDC-UP program (to provide welfare for two-parent families, which previously had been a state option) if one parent in these families would be required to participate in at least sixteen hours of community work experience (CWEP) per week. The Reagan administration was strongly opposed to mandating AFDC-UP, since it would increase the AFDC caseloads, but it was willing to accept the program in exchange for mandatory work provisions.

However, the NGA was opposed to workfare, because it would significantly increase states' costs in administering AFDC. According to Governor Kean, workfare "could actually prolong [a two-parent family's] stay on the rolls, and would, in many cases, be an inappropriate and inefficient use of resources that would be better used in other education and training activities."[47] Governor Clinton also spoke out against the workfare provisions, calling community work experience "makework," an opinion that appears to have changed since he became president. Despite the governors' opposition, the Dole amendment was added to the bill and was crucial to its passage on June 16, 1988. Democrats in the Senate had no choice but to accept the amendment, knowing Reagan would not sign a bill that did not include mandatory work provisions.

The matter was taken up again in conference, where House conferees tried unsuccessfully to eliminate the workfare provisions. Although the governors had been vocal in their aversion to the work requirements, as the bill proceeded to conference, they backed down. As one association staffer put it, "Nobody wanted to send a bill to the President that he would veto. So the compromises were made, the deals were struck." The governors, as well as House Democrats, realized that they would have to accept workfare or give up the bill.

Participation Rates

The White House also wanted to ensure that as many welfare recipients as possible participated in JOBS, the employment and training program in the Senate bill. In order to do so, the administration proposed that a certain percentage of clients in each state be required to participate in JOBS. Initially, the White House wanted to set the rate at 70%. The final bill had a 7% participation rate for the first year, moving to 20% by 1995. The governors opposed the participation rates because, according to one respondent, "The fear was that if states somehow started having to meet participation rates . . . the intensity of work would drop, and people would be put into sort of make-work jobs—job search, CWEP kinds of activities. States would shy away from the intensive education and training components because they were penalized if they didn't make their performance measures."

However, as with workfare provisions, the governors made their position known and then backed down when they realized that Republicans would not pass and Reagan would not sign a bill without participation rates. The governors geared their strategies to the legislative climate. Since they had made *passage* of a welfare reform bill a legislative priority, rather than any particular provision, they were willing to accept some provisions which they did not like. The better a group is at anticipating the reactions and expectations of congressional leaders and committee members, the more likely that group is to achieve legislative success.[48] By understanding what was unacceptable to Republicans and adjusting their strategy accordingly, the governors were being pragmatic actors.

Although the NGA "lost" on participation rates and workfare, they did so knowing it was the only way to get a bill. According to Ray Scheppach, director of the NGA, "We don't really like the participation rates or the work requirement, but we recognize they are necessary to get a bill signed."[49] What the governors really wanted was a federally funded employment and training program, and they were willing to accept participation rates, workfare and an unfavorable "match" to get it. In addition, the governors were happy with the fact that the federal government would fund day care and transitional Medicaid.

Other Government Groups' Activities

The National Governors Association was by far the most influential of the government groups. According to all respondents, the U.S. Conference of Mayors and the National League of Cities played little if any role in welfare reform because welfare is administered at the county, not city, level. Although they, like NGA, NCSL and NACO, testified at congressional hearings, they did not actively lobby on any provision in particular or for the bill in general. NACO and NCSL were slightly more active. Both of these allied with the NGA, and generally let the governors speak for them. Neither media reports nor respondents mentioned NACO or NCSL as being significantly involved in any particular provision.

LEGITIMATION

The Family Support Act was signed by President Reagan on October 13, 1988. It included a new employment and training program with state participation rates, federally funded child care for participants in the program, AFDC-UP with mandatory work requirement, beefed-up child support enforcement provisions, and transitional child care and Medicaid benefits for persons leaving AFDC. The NGA did not get everything it wanted, but it had a new employment and training program, and new federal funds for supportive services. According to all respondents, as well as most newspaper accounts, the governors were very pleased with the bill, and had a significant impact on its passage. More liberal groups were not as happy; they felt that the bill was too "watered-down" and did not go far enough in actually reforming the system. The biggest loss for the advocacy groups was that the bill did not contain provisions for a minimum national benefit. They also did not like the mandatory work requirements or the participation rates.

Respondent Perception of Impact

Respondents were asked to list the most influential interest groups and then rank them on a scale of one (very low impact) to 10 (very high impact). A summary of the results is included in Table 5.1. Not surprisingly, the NGA has the highest rating. In addition, the NGA has the highest rating of any government group in child care, housing and welfare reform legislation. APWA and CDF are also rated highly. NACO and NCSL fall in the middle, while NLC and USCM, which were not significantly involved in the legislation, received the lowest ratings.

The National Governors' Association was involved in the legislation from the beginning of the process, and worked closely with Congress to develop a bill that would be acceptable to the administration. Almost all of the respondents said that a bill could not have passed without the NGA. Some clarified that and said that while NGA support was important, the lobbying of individual governors was crucial. Generally, if NGA withholds its support, a bill cannot pass. With NGA's support, passage is not necessarily ensured. But with the active involvement of several governors, members of Congress felt some pressure to pass welfare legislation, which appeared to have broad support. One respondent noted that John Sununu, who was chair of the NGA in 1988, did not personally agree with the governors' policy on the welfare reform bill, but that he supported the bill anyway. He "felt that it was his job to represent the governors and he did."

Table 5.1 Ratings of Interest Group Impact on Welfare Reform Legislation

National Governors' Association	8.7
American Public Welfare Association	7.5
Children's Defense Fund	6.9
National Conference of State Legislatures	4.0
National Association of Counties	4.0
U. S. Conference of Mayors	1.0
National League of Cities	1.0

Scores are averages of respondents' ratings of interest group impact. "10" means very high impact; "1" very low impact.

Several respondents mentioned APWA and CDF as being among the more or less "permanent lobby" for welfare reform. These groups are more client-oriented, and much more liberal, than the NGA. APWA in particular was lobbying for a case management approach to welfare that would encourage self-sufficiency. The group's biggest issue was to get a national minimum benefit. But, as one respondent noted, the members of APWA (public welfare administrators) are employed by the members of NGA. So the group was somewhat constrained in its lobbying efforts because it did not want to be seen as being too far afield of the NGA. CDF was somewhat less involved in welfare reform. Issues such as child support enforcement and extended day care benefits were important to the group, but the legislation was more specifically directed at welfare clients. CDF and APWA were involved in lobbying, but it was really the governors who pushed the issue.

Not all respondents were willing to answer the question on impact using specific numbers. Respondents who would not rate the groups talked more generally about groups' concerns in the legislation and involvement in its passage. They said that it was too difficult to assign numbers to the groups' activities, but even those who did not rate the groups said the NGA had the greatest impact on the bill and that it could not have passed without the governors. Both congressional and association respondents had difficulty with the question. For those association staff who did not answer, it may have been because the groups (other than NGA) were not directly involved in the legislation. On the other hand, congressional staff may not have wanted to take credit away from their own (or their senators' or representatives') work on the bill.

Group Positions on Specific Provisions

Table 5.2 lists some major provisions of the legislation as passed, and whether the groups were in favor of that particular provision, opposed or did not have a strong lobbying position. It is evident from the table that none of the groups got legislation that was completely consistent with their preferences. Although NGA was unhappy with participation rates and mandatory work requirements, the group ended up with the best wins-to-losses ratio (5 to 2). CDF and APWA both had win/loss ratios of 3/3, so they fared less well than NCSL, which was rated lower by respondents but had a 3/2 win/loss ratio. This is probably because CDF and APWA command more media and congressional attention than NCSL, so their input on welfare reform was better known. In addition, NCSL tends to be a more moderate organization, so its group positions tend to be those that are more easily supported in Congress. APWA and CDF command attention in part because they are so liberal. And because they promote more liberal policies, they are likely to fight for issues that have little chance of passing. The local groups, especially USCM and NLC, did not take a strong lobbying position on several of the issues. This is consistent with the fact that respondents rated them very low on impact.

It was clear from responses to interview questions that both congressional and association staff rated NGA very highly, not because of its stand on specific provisions, but because the organization was pushing for welfare reform in general. Many respondents mentioned the willingness of the NGA to compromise, and several had to think for a few minutes before they could come up with any provision that the governors might consider a loss. The governors did not stake out immovable positions, and it was apparent that they were willing to settle for less than what they initially wanted in order to get a bill the President could sign. Because they concentrated on passage in general, respondents tended to forget the specifics that the governors had asked for. Almost every respondent said the NGA's biggest success was the passage of the bill.

CONCLUSIONS

NGA acted differently in some ways than Haider would have expected. For one thing, the group was both an initiator and a facilitator. Additionally, the group members were perceived as being the experts in welfare reform policy, and thus the group carried weight beyond its public official status. The fact that states had implemented welfare reform efforts through the WIN program gave the NGA an advantage in expertise, where Haider would have expected other

Table 5.2 State and Local Government Groups' Positions on
Legislative Provisions (Welfare Reform)

	APWA	CDF	NGA	NACO	NCSL	USCM	NLC
Minimum Benefits	-	-	+/-	0	+	+	0
Participation Rates	-	-	-	-	-	-	-
Mandatory Work Requirements	-	-	-	0	0	-	0
Child Support Enforcement	+	+	+	+	+	+	+
AFDC-UP	+	+	+	+	-	0	0
Funding Match	0	0	+/-	+/-	0	0	0
Transitional Benefits	+	+	+	+	+	0	+

+   Provision is consistent with stated group policy
-   Provision is in opposition to state group policy
0   Group did not take a strong lobbying position
+/- Provision is partially consistent with group policy

groups to have this advantage. "The government groups generally compete at a disadvantage with the more well-established claimants which tend to be more cohesive and possess greater expertise in special areas of public policy."[50]

The welfare reform bill falls into Haider's first classification of legislation, minimal conflict. The state and local groups were not opposed to each other, and in fact the government groups let NGA concentrate on this issue. Although the state and local groups did not agree on all provisions of the legislation, there were no major conflicts. Since a welfare program was already in existence, there was no fear of moving benefits from one level of government to another.

The governors were the most active lobbying group among the state and locals. The group used the tactics that Haider described. The governors nourished their allies by helping develop compromises and giving up some things (participation rates, mandatory work) that they would have preferred. They counted heads and money, helping to get the votes necessary for passage in the House, and concentrating lobbying efforts on the funding match in the legislation. They used research to get the subject on the agenda, particularly results from WIN demonstration studies.

NOTES

1. U.S. Congress, Senate, Committee on Finance, *Welfare Reform or Replacement (Child Support Enforcement). Hearings before the Subcommittee on Social Security and Family Policy*, 100th Cong., 1st sess., 1987.

2. See Haider, *When Governments Come to Washington*, p. 214.

3. See Daniel Patrick Moynihan, *The Politics of a Guaranteed Income: The Nixon Administration and the Family Assistance Plan* (New York: Random House, 1973).

4. "Welfare Reform: Big Proposals, Small Fixes," *Congressional Quarterly Weekly Report*, September 27, 1986, p. 2285.

5. Ibid.

6. Quoted in Julie Rovner, "Welfare Reform: The Next Domestic Priority?" *Congressional Quarterly Weekly Report*, September 27, 1987, p. 2281.

7. Charles Murray, *Losing Ground: American Social Policy 1950-1980* (New York: Basic Books, 1984).

8. See Sheldon Danziger and David Weinberg, *Fighting Poverty, What Works and What Doesn't* (Cambridge, Mass.: Harvard University Press, 1986); also John Schwarz, *America's Hidden Success: A Reassessment of Public Policy from Kennedy to Reagan* (New York: Norton, 1988).

9. Michael Novak et al., *The New Consensus on Family and Welfare: A Community of Self-Reliance* (Washington: American Enterprise Institute for Public Policy Research, 1987).

10. Task Force on Poverty and Welfare, New York State, *A New Social Contract: Rethinking the Nature and Purpose of Public Assistance* (Albany: Executive Chamber, Task Force on Poverty and Welfare, 1986).

11. U.S. Congress, Senate, Committee on Finance, *Welfare Reform or Replacement*, p. 192.

12. Census Bureau figures, quoted in *Congressional Quarterly Weekly Report*, September 27, 1986, p. 2282.

13. Judith Gueron, *Reforming Welfare with Work*, Occasional Paper 2 (New York: Ford Foundation Project on Social Welfare and the American Future, 1987).

14. See Demetra Nightingale, *Evaluation of the Massachusetts Employment and Training Choices Program* (Washington: The Urban Institute, 1990), and June O'Neill, *Work and Welfare in Massachusetts: An Evaluation of the ET Program* (Boston: Pioneer Institute for Public Policy Research, 1990).

15. Sanford F. Schram, "The New Federalism and Social Welfare: AFDC in the Midwest," in Peter Eisinger and William Gormley, eds., *The Midwest Response to the New Federalism* (Madison: University of Wisconsin Press, 1988), pp. 264–292.

16. Julie Rovner, "Governors Jump-Start Welfare Reform Drive," *Congressional Quarterly Weekly Report*, February 28, 1987, p. 376.

17. Erica Baum, "When the Witch Doctors Agree: The Family Support Act and Social Science Research," *Journal of Policy Analysis and Management* 10 (1991): 603–615.

18. U.S. Congress, House, Democratic Caucus, "The Road to Independence: Strengthening America's Families in Need" (Washington: House Democratic Caucus, July 30, 1986).

19. Ben W. Heineman, Jr., "Time for Welfare Reform: Everyone Agrees Work Is the Answer, but What's the Question?" *Washington Post*, February 15, 1987, sec. C, p. 2.

20. American Public Welfare Association, *Case Management and Welfare Reform* (Washington: American Public Welfare Association, July 31, 1987).

21. U.S. Congress, Senate, Committee on Finance, *Welfare Reform or Replacement,* 100th Cong., 1st sess., 1987.

22. Spencer Rich, "Reagan Welfare Proposal Criticized by Agencies," *Washington Post*, February 10, 1987, sec. A, p. 8.

23. Only one governor, Wisconsin's Republican Tommy G. Thompson, voted against the proposal, on the grounds that his state already had an expansive welfare program.

24. See statement of Governor Michael N. Castle, U.S Congress, Senate, Committee on Finance, *Welfare Reform or Replacement*; also David S. Broder, "Governors Endorse Welfare Overhaul," *Washington Post,* February 25, 1987, sec A, p. 3, and Rovner, *Congressional Quarterly Weekly Report*, February 28, 1987, p. 376.

25. Quoted in Rovner, *Congressional Quarterly Weekly Report*, February 28, 1987, p. 376.

26. Julie Rovner, "Governors Press Reagan, Bentsen on Welfare," *Congressional Quarterly Weekly Report*, February 27, 1988, p. 512.

27. AFDC-UP (AFDC for families with unemployed parents) provided benefits, at state option, to two-parent families.

28. Both are quoted in Julie Rovner, "Reagan Team Tears into Democrats Welfare Plan," *Congressional Quarterly Weekly Report*, April 4, 1987, p. 627.

29. Quoted in Robert Pear, "Sweeping Welfare Revision Plan Stresses Responsibility of Parents," *New York Times*, July 19, 1987, p. 21.

30. Julie Rovner, *Congressional Quarterly Weekly Report*, February 28, 1987, p. 376.

31. Edwin M. Yoder, Jr., "Listen to Moynihan on Kids in Poverty," *Washington Post*, July 28, 1987, sec. A, p. 15.

32. Julie Rovner, "Congress Clears Overhaul of Welfare System," *Congressional Quarterly Weekly Report*, October 1, 1988, p. 2699.

33. Haider, *When Governments Come to Washington*, p. 229.

34. Statement of Governor Michael N. Castle, U.S. Congress, Senate, Committee on Finance, *Welfare Reform or Replacement*.

35. Harold Ford was indicted on bank, tax and mail fraud charges in mid-1987 and was forced to give up his chair of the Subcommittee on Public Assistance and Unemployment Compensation.

36. Haider, *When Governments Come to Washington*, p. 237.

37. Testimony of Governor William Clinton on behalf of the NGA, U.S. Congress, House, Committee on Education and Labor, *Hearings on Welfare Reform: HR 30, Fair Work Opportunities Act of 1970 and HR 1720, Family Welfare Reform Act of 1987*, 100th Congress, 1st sess., 1987.

38. Ibid.

39. Alicia Smith, quoted in Rovner, *Congressional Quarterly Weekly Report*, September 27, 1986, p. 2284.

40. *Washington Post*, December 10, 1987, sec. A, p. 27.

41. Patrick L. Knudsen, "After Long, Bruising Battle, House Approves Welfare Bill," *Congressional Quarterly Weekly Report*, December 19, 1987, p. 3157.

42. Ibid., p. 3159.

43. Haider, *When Governments Come to Washington*, p. 245.

44. Ibid., p. 232.

45. Rovner, *Congressional Quarterly Weekly Report*, February 27, 1988, p. 512.

46. Quoted in Rovner, *Congressional Quarterly Weekly Report*, February 27, 1988, p. 513.

47. Quoted in Julie Rovner, "Deep Schisms Still Imperil Welfare Overhaul," *Congressional Quarterly Weekly Report*, June 18, 1988, p. 1650.

48. Haider, *When Governments Come to Washington*, p. 244.

49. Quoted in Julie Rovner, "Welfare Conferees Narrow Their Differences," *Congressional Quarterly Weekly Report*, August 6, 1988, p. 2202.

50. Haider, *When Governments Come to Washington*, p. 226.

Chapter 6

State and Local Interest Groups as Lobbyists in the Federal System

THE FOURTH PHASE OF INTERGOVERNMENTAL LOBBYING

State and local government interest groups began acting as lobbying organizations during the New Deal. The first phase of intergovernmental lobbying, from then until the early 1960s, saw an increase in the prestige of urban mayors, as well as an increase in federal grants to cities. In the second phase, from the early 1960s to about 1969, the states and localities began vying with each other for federal grants. By the third phase (from about 1960 to about 1979), the groups had established themselves as prominent lobbying organizations, and claimed revenue sharing as a policy success.[1] Donald Haider studied the lobbying effectiveness of the first three phases (concentrating on the second phase) and found that the governmental lobbies had access to the federal government and were effective on relatively narrow policy questions. The first two phases were characterized by increasing federal spending and increasing "strings" (requirements) attached to that spending. The third phase, during the Nixon administration, gave the states and localities exactly what they wanted: more money with fewer strings attached.

Since Haider's study, the policy environment has changed considerably. In the three phases that Haider describes, the federal grant system was expanding. Because states and localities are concerned with spatial issues (e.g., what government level has authority in funding and administration of programs), such a political environment is favorable to their desires. As federal grants expand, states and localities receive more money. The fourth phase differs from all three of the previous phases because the federal grant system began declining after 1979. Such a decline leads to an economic environment which is hostile to the desires of the states and local groups.

The political environment also changed in the fourth phase of lobbying. Both Carter and Reagan were opposed to "big government," and Reagan attempted to give states and localities increased responsibility for domestic programs, in the hope that eventually all levels of government would abandon pursuit of the liberal social policies that the Great Society had created. The Reagan administration was ideologically opposed to social welfare programs, the very programs for which Hays predicts the government groups would turn to the federal government. The political environment changed somewhat after Reagan left office. President Bush was less stringent and less ideological in his opposition to new social programs, and Congress, which went along with Reagan (at least in the early years of his presidency), was less threatened by the Bush administration.

The political environment throughout the fourth phase has generally been hostile to increased government social spending and, at the same time, responsive to state and local calls for increased authority. An unusual window of opportunity opened in the late 1980s, when Congress, responding to the end of the Reagan presidency, pushed for new social programs, and the "kinder, gentler" administration of President Bush went along. This may have been the last chance for state and local groups to get new or expanded federal grants. Since the early 1990s, the political environment has been conducive to decreasing federal requirements on the state and local governments (particularly with the passage of legislation restricting unfunded mandates). The end of the Reagan presidency also marked an increased prestige for the National Governors' Association. Although Reagan wanted states to take over responsibility for social programs, he had a negative view of the state and local groups, which he considered to be interested only in increasing federal government spending. Starting at the end of Reagan's term, the governors' expertise at implementing welfare programs and their role as the chief executives of states has strengthened the NGA's position. The election of President Clinton, a former NGA leader, has also raised the prestige of the association.

The political environment became somewhat more favorable to the state and local groups in the late 1980s, but the economic environment by that time had created new problems that have persisted throughout the 1990s. The federal deficit and state fiscal crises have constrained both federal and state spending. This economic environment presents great difficulties for states and localities. The subnational governments are responsible for providing services needed by constituents experiencing economic hardship, but they are finding it increasingly difficult to pay for such services. As Hays has demonstrated, such a situation leads the government groups to lobby the federal government, but the federal government is constrained in its abilities to pay for new programs.

This fourth phase is obviously quite different from the three phases that Haider described, and warrants a new examination of the lobbying efforts of the state and local groups. If they were effective when the policy, political and economic environments were favorable to them, how have they fared when one or more of these environments is hostile to their desires?

THE STATE AND LOCAL GROUPS AS LOBBYISTS

Overall Influence of State and Local Groups

In addition to questions about the government groups' impact on each of the bills, respondents were asked to rate their overall influence in Congress. Respondents were read a list of the five government lobbying groups, and were told to rate them on a scale of one (very little influence) to ten (very high influence).

Table 6.1 shows the average ratings for respondents on general (rather than legislation-specific) influence. The NGA, which came out on top in child care and welfare reform but not housing, was at the head of the list in terms of general influence. It received the highest average rating from both congressional and association respondents. Comparing association staff ratings of state and local group influence to congressional staff ratings, it is interesting to note that each state and local group got a higher average rating from association staff than from congressional staff, with the exception of the NGA. The NGA got higher ratings from congressional respondents than from association staff. Association respondents believed that the NGA receives more attention for its activities than other state and local groups, but that the other groups are instrumental in providing information to congressional staff.

The NGA is the best-known of the state and local groups because its members command more attention. While the other groups have large and unwieldy memberships, there are only fifty governors, all of whom find it relatively easy to gain media and public attention. Since state governorships have become a route to the White House, many governors cultivate media coverage. Because of this, governors are often called on to give testimony before congressional committees. In addition, the NGA has the largest budget of any of the groups.[2] Also, the emphasis on enhancing the role of the states in the system of federalism gives the NGA increased prestige.

USCM, NLC and NCSL fall behind NGA, but are close to each other. NACO is far behind all of the other groups. Counties are the entities that are at the front lines of social programs, so it would seem that they would be heavily involved in lobbying for social programs, and thus perceived as more influential. NACO, however, has not been a strong lobbying organization. Its members are less well-known, and those who testify before Congress are seen

Table 6.1 Perceptions of General Influence of State and Local
Government Groups

	All Respondents	Congressional Respondents	Association Respondents
NGA	7.4	7.5	7.2
USCM	6.0	5.6	6.8
NLC	5.9	5.8	6.0
NCSL	5.8	5.3	6.3
NACO	5.0	4.5	5.4

Scores are averages of respondents' ratings of interest group impact. "10" means very high impact;
"1" very low impact.

as representing their particular county rather than NACO as a whole. In
contrast, NLC has some better-known and more activist members. For example,
Mayor Jim Moran of Alexandria, now a representative from Virginia's eighth
congressional district, was an outspoken president of NLC in the late 1980s. In
addition, both NACO and NCSL were much more highly rated by association
staff than by congressional staff. Association staff are more familiar with the
work of the two groups; NCSL in particular is noted among the interest groups
for its research abilities. Also, Senate respondents are not as familiar with
NCSL and NACO, which concentrate their lobbying efforts on the House.

Comparison of the Three Acts

One government group, the National Governors' Association, played a
significant role in the passage of the Family Support Act, both in agenda-setting
and in policy formulation. The Act for Better Child Care had somewhat less
input from state and local groups, although the governors again played a
significant role. The National Affordable Housing Act had the least involvement
by state and locals, and local groups had more impact than state groups. Child
care became part of the agenda because of pressure from advocacy groups;
housing rose to the top of the agenda because of congressional concerns about
the issue; the Family Support Act came out of state experiences in welfare
reform as well as a stated commitment on the part of the President and Senator

Moynihan to reform the system. The bill least affected by the government groups was the National Affordable Housing Act. It was necessary to get the state and local groups' support to ensure passage, but they were not the most influential in the bill. Congress was much more "proactive" on housing. Local groups were more important than state groups on this bill's passage; they had a significant impact on the funding split and appropriations. USCM and NLC had the highest ratings among the government groups (see Table 4.1). Along with NACO, they were the most active of the groups. However, even though NGA was less active than NACO, it got a similar rating for impact on housing legislation (5.1 and 5.0 respectively). NGA is better-known and respected in Congress than NACO, which one respondent said had an image problem in Congress. The government groups were not facilitators in housing legislation. The groups were less concerned about mediating compromises than they were about ensuring that governmental entities got sufficient funding.

In contrast, the state and local groups were facilitators in child care legislation. Although the CDF/ABC coalition was the initiator for the legislation, without the NGA the bill would not have passed. The state groups were more active and effective than local groups. The NGA used access effectively to eliminate standards provisions from the legislation. The NCSL exploited cleavages to ensure that the legislation would contain a new grant rather than an expanded entitlement program.

The Family Support Act was most significantly impacted by a government group. The NGA strongly supported a welfare reform bill, and, in an unusual role for a government group, acted as an initiator for the legislation. Activist governors were willing to lobby for the bill, and the group was more amenable to compromise than other state and local groups. NGA used its access and legitimacy and concentrated its lobbying on one-on-one contact with members of Congress. NGA was really the driving force behind welfare reform; the other groups were less involved.

TESTING HYPOTHESES

Hypothesis 1: State and local interest groups are more likely to be effective when they act together.

In child care and housing legislation, this hypothesis appears to be somewhat true. However, the governors acted on their own for welfare reform, the legislation on which they had the most impact.

State and local groups formed informal alliances on three issues in the child care debate: national standards, the ABC grant program vs. the Title XX increases and local issues. NCSL and NGA worked together with the Bush administration on the national standards compromise; their efforts proved successful, and respondents as well as media accounts credited the groups with the final compromise, although NGA was almost universally perceived as having had more impact than NCSL on eliminating standards. NCSL and NACO, and to a lesser degree USCM and NLC, joined together to back a grant program instead of Title XX earmarked increases. Although they won on this issue, most respondents did not give the groups credit for the final compromise. The ABC coalition and Democratic Senators also favored a grant program. The state and local groups added to the voices clamoring for ABC grants. On local issues, the local groups lost. They were not considered strong lobbies, and their interests were laid aside over Republican concerns that the legislation created a new bureaucracy.

Several issues were important to the state and local groups in housing legislation: matching, HOME, HOPE, full-funding and the state local funding split. The groups were partially successful on two of those issues (HOME and full-funding), but unsuccessful on matching and HOPE. The local groups' biggest success was in the funding split; they acted in a coalition with each other but against the states, who were not as active on the issue. In this legislation, the groups were pitted against each other on one of their most important issues, the funding split. On their other important issue, full-funding for the legislation, the groups acted in a successful coalition.

In welfare legislation, the NGA acted alone, and received the highest rating of any government group in any of the three case studies. The other groups were generally in support of welfare reform legislation, but their lobbying was limited. Where they agreed with the governors' positions, they let the governors speak for them. The governors were in the forefront of this issue, but they also were not opposed by any of the other state and local groups. Their success appears to be due to the fact that not only were the governors able to command media attention, they were willing to do so, and they were acting in an area where consensus among governmental actors was already building.

The state and local groups were able to present a more united front on welfare and child care legislation. The NGA was in the forefront on both of these issues, and the other groups, with some exceptions, were willing to let the NGA speak for them. There was more disagreement among the groups over housing legislation, and the perception among congressional staff members was that the groups were bickering over the funding issue. The coalitions that were formed pitted state groups against local groups. The state and local groups were rated lowest on impact for housing, the legislation on which there was the least agreement among the groups.

It appears that the existence of a coalition among the state and local groups is not necessarily important for them to be effective on legislation. There was no formal coalition among state and local groups for welfare reform, yet the NGA received a very high rating for impact on this legislation. What seems to be more important is that the groups not demonstrate substantial disagreement over major aspects of the legislation. Although there was some difference of opinion among the groups on both child care and welfare reform legislation (e.g., the Title XX issue in child care), the groups concentrated their lobbying efforts on those issues on which they agreed. In contrast, the state and local groups lobbied most ardently on the funding split for housing legislation, the one area in which their views were strongly divided. Consequently, congressional and association perception of impact was much lower.

Hypothesis 2: State and local groups are more likely to be effective when they act in a coalition with other interest groups.

The state and local groups did not ally themselves with other groups to a significant extent in any of the three cases. Even though there were coalitions involved in each act, the state and local groups tended to distance themselves from the coalitions. For example, although the state and local groups were informally aligned with the ABC coalition, according to one respondent, "they never let the coalition speak for them," because "the state and local groups know what it's like to be beholden to interest groups." Their distance from the ABC coalition probably aided in their legitimacy, particularly when CDF lost favor among many congressional actors.

The state and local groups also acted separately from other groups on housing legislation. They lobbied in an informal coalition with other groups on the issue of a block grant for HOME, for which the coalition was successful. However, the state and local groups did not lobby extensively themselves, preferring to let the housing coalition speak for them. In addition, it is difficult to attribute the HOME program to any interest group, because it was a quid pro quo for the Democrats to pass a housing bill.

The NGA acted in a relatively separate sphere from other interest groups for welfare reform. APWA and CDF were also lobbying for welfare reform legislation, and the groups acted in an informal coalition, but when the compromises were struck and the bargains were made, the governors were acting on behalf of the NGA and the states, not a coalition of interest groups. Unlike in child care or housing, NGA, as the lead group placing the issue on the agenda, did not represent an umbrella organization of interest groups.

Coalitions of interest groups were important to the passage of child care and housing legislation; however, the government groups were not significantly involved in these coalitions. What was important was not so much that a coalition existed, but that there was evidence of broad-based support for the legislation. In welfare reform, where alliances were less formal, there were strong indications that a large number of individuals and groups were in favor of legislation; in child care and housing, the coalitions demonstrated a demand for change. Coalitions appear to be most useful at the agenda-setting phase of the process, where, for example, the ABC coalition could push Congress to action. During consideration of a bill, however, coalitions appear to be less important, and the fact that the government groups were separate from the ABC coalition may have given them increased clout during policy formulation. Likewise, the fact that the NGA was acting alone in many respects on welfare reform made it possible for the group to develop compromises in Congress.

Hypothesis 3: State groups are more effective in the Senate; local groups are more effective in the House.

Overall the governors had more access in the Senate than any of the other groups. For example, one house staffer declared that Senate staff would "put the Governors next to the right hand of God." However, this access also carried over, at least to some degree, to the House. In addition, the only other state group, the National Conference of State Legislatures, did not have increased access in the Senate. As a matter of fact, the group was better connected to the House than the Senate, because, according to one respondent, many representatives are former state legislators. Respondents from the House side routinely mentioned that the governors were more important in the Senate, and many respondents said representatives and their staffs listen to the local groups.

Within child care legislation, the NGA was most effective in the Senate on the issue of national standards, while the NCSL had more impact in the House on the issue of the grant program. In housing, the issue on which local groups were most successful came up in the Senate. The Senate bill contained block grant language, and the local groups were able to change the funding split from 50-50 to 60-40 in a Senate committee before the bill went to conference. Of course, the Senators' relationship with the governors may explain why the local groups were not completely successful in getting the 70-30 local-state split. In addition, the Senate bill included the HOME block grant, which was more important to the state and local groups than the bill introduced by Gonzalez in the House. Most of the action on the bill was in the Senate, so it is difficult to compare the role of the groups in the two houses.

The governors were highly successful on welfare reform legislation in the House, where they enjoyed unprecedented access, and were able to broker deals during committee and subcommittee consideration. In addition, the governors were crucial in vote-counting and arm-twisting, particularly of Southern Democrats, to get legislation passed in the House. It appears that the governors got less of what they wanted from the Senate, which, as the more conservative of the two chambers, was more concerned with getting legislation consistent with Republican administration preferences. This is not to say that the governors did not enjoy access to the Senate; they did, but the House was more amenable to their policy ideas.

Although the NGA appears to have more access in the Senate than the other groups, the groups' effectiveness on various provisions was not limited to one house or the other. In housing, the local groups were most successful on the funding split, which came up in the Senate, and the governors were quite successful with brokering compromise and garnering votes for welfare reform in the House.

Hypothesis 4: The tactics of state and local groups are similar to those of other interest groups.

The difference between tactics of the government and other interest groups was evident in consideration of the ABC bill. For this legislation, the state and local groups used more conciliatory tactics than did the ABC coalition. Their tactics tended to be direct: testifying and personally contacting members of Congress.[3] The ABC alliance used more indirect methods, attracting media attention, and organizing massive grassroots mobilization. The government groups' tactics did not alienate members of Congress the way CDF's did. Congressional respondents had a more favorable attitude toward the government groups at the end of the process, which may mean more possibility for future successes for the groups.

There was less difference among interest groups in lobbying for housing legislation. The government interest groups and the other interest groups used direct tactics: testifying and personally contacting members of Congress. There was less use of media than for child care legislation, where the CDF distinguished itself from the state and local groups by attracting a large amount of media attention and mobilizing a grassroots constituency. For housing, the government groups were the ones that mobilized the grassroots for the full-funding issue, and one respondent said that whenever a mayor or governor testifies, the media covers the hearings. Thus, for this legislation, the state and local groups attracted more media attention than did the other interest groups involved.

Similarly, for welfare reform, the government interest groups and the other interest groups both used direct tactics. The governors used the media more in this legislation than in the other two acts. For example, Clinton courted and received publicity when he testified before Congress or met with the administration; he also wrote an editorial for the *Washington Post* in favor of welfare reform. In addition, once the media believed welfare reform had momentum, and the governors were responsible for it, they covered the governors' activities on the issue. The media reports added to the sense of inevitability for the passage of welfare reform.

Overall, the government groups use much the same tactics as other interest groups. However, they shy away from publicity on controversial issues. The

NGA would not publicly support the mega-block grant in housing legislation, because such support, while in the governors' interests, would undermine efforts of members of Congress who had been working on housing for three years. The NGA also backed down on its support of the Stenholm-Shaw substitute for child care legislation, because many of their Democratic allies in Congress were adamantly opposed. The main difference in tactics between the government groups (especially the NGA) and other public interest groups is that other groups are generally more strident advocates for a particular issue area. Because the government groups are interested in a variety of issues and preoccupied with spatial concerns, they tend to look for ways to generate compromise.

Hypothesis 5: The state and local interest groups have more access than other interest groups.

This appears to be true at least to a degree. State and local groups, especially the NGA, are able to get the attention of members of Congress and their staff, and while they may not win on every issue, they seem to have more access than other groups. The governors negotiated with the Senate and the White House on the issue of standards in child care, and individual NCSL members were almost always able to meet with their representatives. The governors had a remarkable amount of access in both the House and the Senate when working on welfare reform. The fact that Governor Clinton was able to participate in the Ways and Means Committee's mark-up demonstrates a level of access not enjoyed by other groups. In addition, because welfare reform had started at the state level, the governors were perceived as "experts." Their expertise appears to have given them more legitimacy than any other group (including other government groups) in the process.

However, in housing legislation, the government groups did not appear to have more access than other interest groups. Because the state and local groups were arguing over who would get the majority of the funding for new housing programs, they were not perceived by congressional staff as being serious players in the debate. Although the government groups were expressing their natural interest in spatial policy, congressional actors saw the debate as trivial. However, even in housing policy, respondents maintained that legislation could not have passed unless the government groups supported it.

Hypothesis 6: The state and local interest groups are more effective on concrete legislative provisions than on abstract issues.

Within each act, the government groups were effective on some concrete issues during the legitimation stage. The NGA was quite effective on the issue of standards in child care; NGA and NCSL were at least somewhat successful in changing the allocation formula for the child care grants. When asked about the impact of the state and local groups on child care legislation, respondents generally pointed to specific legislative "wins." When asked about the impact of the ABC coalition, respondents talked about its broader role in agenda-setting and creating demand for child care legislation.

Similarly, the housing issues on which the government groups were most effective were concrete issues debated during legitimation: the funding split and appropriations (full-funding). However, some of the issues on which they were unsuccessful were also specific and concrete: matching and HOPE. The government groups were not credited with the overall passage of the legislation by any of the respondents. Their success was mentioned in terms of small, incremental changes that occurred after policy formulation.

In contrast, the governors were not as effective on specific provisions in welfare reform. They were unsuccessful on the two issues that were most important to them: participation rates and mandatory work requirements. They lost on these issues because they were willing to compromise them for broader goals: inclusion of federally funded employment and training programs and overall passage of the bill. In this case, the governors were more effective in setting the agenda and formulating policy than in maintaining specific interests during policy formulation. Respondents and news media credit the NGA with getting welfare reform on the agenda and with brokering compromises, but the governors were not as successful on specific provisions.

Interestingly, the NGA was perceived as having a larger impact on welfare reform than any other government group had on any of the three acts, even though the group was less successful on specific provisions (at least those that it considered important). Respondents tended to differentiate between overall impact of the groups on legislation and their success or failure on specific provisions. Respondents believed that welfare reform legislation could not have been passed without the support of the governors, despite the fact that they did not win on all of their goals. As a matter of fact, the fact that the NGA lost on some important provisions made the welfare reform possible. The administration would not have signed any legislation unless it had mandatory work provisions, which the governors opposed. If the NGA had chosen not to support a bill that included such provisions, Congress would have been at an impasse: pass a bill without mandatory work and the bill would be vetoed; include mandatory work and the bill would never pass because it would not get the governors' endorsement. The NGA's willingness to compromise on more narrow issues made overall passage possible.

CONCLUSIONS

For a brief period in the late 1980s, the political environment became more conducive to the passage of new federal social programs. However, the political environment was constrained by the economic environment, and Congress and the administration were reluctant to expand social spending when faced with public concerns over the size of the federal debt. The government groups reacted to the situation by both maintaining their defensive posture and pushing for some new programs. For example, the state and local groups were not significantly involved in placing housing policy on the national agenda, even though the issue affected local, particularly city, governments. When the policy was before Congress, the groups were not as involved in substantive issues as they were in determining how much money each level of government would get. They were defending their turf rather than pressing for reform.

Similarly, although the government groups were more involved in child care legislation than housing, their most significant win was in eliminating standards from the child care bill. The NGA, which was involved in mediating compromises in Congress, fought the hardest on the issue of standards, which the group viewed as a new mandate. The NGA was less involved in the policy after its "win" on standards, and NCSL and NACO lobbied for a new grant program rather than an entitlement program.

The Family Support Act is the only one of the three that was characterized by intensive subnational group lobbying in all phases of the process, including agenda-setting. Interestingly, welfare reform was also the only act that was passed during the Reagan administration. In this case, the NGA was in an offensive rather than defensive posture. The group was lobbying for significant reform and compromised on some important issues to ensure passage of the bill. The groups responded in part to Reagan's call for welfare reform and to research that concluded that work programs could help welfare recipients. The welfare reform debate came late in Reagan's presidency, and interest groups and Congress saw an opening for new social spending when Reagan indicated a willingness to sign some form of welfare reform legislation.

Although welfare legislation was the first significant social spending legislation since the Reagan presidency, it was an exception rather than the beginning of a new era. The NGA was highly successful in this policy area, and went on to be somewhat successful in child care legislation. However, the governors have not taken on a similar role in any legislation since the Family Support Act. In the 1995 debates over welfare, the NGA took a low profile, mostly because Democratic and Republican governors could not agree on ending the entitlement status of welfare.[4] (Changing welfare from an entitlement to a block grant would theoretically give states more leeway in administering welfare, but it would mean a fixed amount of money for the program.) Even after the 1988 bill was passed, the governors experienced some difficulties in implementation, both because the regulations promulgated by the administration interpreted the legislation more narrowly than the governors expected, and because recession led to swollen AFDC rolls which strained the capacities of the states to provide employment and training programs to recipients.

The state and local groups today face the same internal constraints and have the same characteristics that Haider described. It is difficult to achieve group consensus because membership is diverse. The governors are still an association of fifty prima donnas. The Conference of Mayors is still largely Democratic. The groups have professional staffs, and are perceived to be more legitimate than other groups by congressional staff. The groups today face a big external constraint that was not present at the time of Haider's study: the federal deficit, which limits federal spending on grant programs for states and localities.

The groups are in some ways less effective than at the time of Haider's study. For example, housing legislation, which was at one time the domain of the USCM, was least impacted by state and local groups among the three acts. The direct federal-city connection is loosened, and the local groups thus have less clout. On the other hand, the NGA appears to be gaining more clout than the other groups, as is evidenced by their high rating for overall influence among the respondents, and the credit that the group received for its role in welfare reform. The groups are less effective when competing with each other (as in housing legislation) and more effective when there appears to be a groundswell of support for legislation (child care and welfare).

Throughout the fourth phase of intergovernmental lobbying, there has been an emphasis on increasing the role of the states in the federal system. This has increased the prestige of the governors, who are now not only important in their own right, but also as experts in the provision of social programs. The NGA consciously used that expertise in lobbying for welfare reform in 1988. The group was able to achieve consensus on that issue, because it was lobbying for a program expansion. As the 104th Congress considers returning authority over social programs to the states, the NGA has more difficulty achieving consensus. Republican and Democratic governors alike want more authority, but Democratic governors in particular are fearful that increased authority may come at the expense of sufficient funding. If the NGA cannot achieve consensus, then their lobbying power is significantly diminished. In addition, congressional policymakers have difficulty in defending programs that return power to the states if the states do not agree on the merits of such programs.

It is possible that we are entering a fifth phase of intergovernmental lobbying. The political environment changed in 1992 with the election of a Democratic president. Clinton, as a centrist Democrat, is not so much ideologically opposed to increased government social spending as he is fiscally restrained in such spending. Since becoming president, he has moved to the right, particularly with respect to welfare reform. His welfare reform proposals have focused on time-limiting benefits and requiring community service work for those recipients who cannot find jobs. Such proposals are much more conservative than the legislation he supported as lobbyist for the NGA, but not as conservative as the block grant proposals before the 104th Congress. Moving him further to the right is the constraint of a new Republican-majority Congress, which is both fiscally and ideologically opposed to new social spending, and supportive of a system of federalism which gives increased authority to the states.

The government groups are quite different from other interest groups. Groups such as CDF are more ideological and issue-oriented than the state and local groups; they are really advocacy groups. The state and local groups are most concerned with their spatial interests. Other government groups such as APWA and NAHRO are interested in functional concerns, and are more limited in the policies they pursue (e.g. welfare or housing). An interesting change between the fourth phase and the first three is that the spatial role of the groups has taken on increased importance. Presidents throughout the fourth phase have focused on reinvigorating federalism and giving states more authority. The groups have taken advantage of that focus. As long as there is consensus within and among the groups, they can proclaim that a program is better run at the state and local levels than at the federal level, and national policymakers are likely to agree. While Haider found that groups had to adjust their spatial interests to the functional concerns of congressional actors, such adjustments are less important in a time period when decentralizing the federal system is the emphasis.

If inter or intra-group divisions are evident, the state and local groups achieve less lobbying success. When the state and local groups disagreed over the funding split in housing legislation, congressional actors thought the groups were focusing on a trivial issue. The level of government which receives program funding will never be trivial to state and local groups, whose interests are more spatial than functional. But if their spatial interests cause inter-group divisions, policymakers will be unable to take the groups' concerns seriously. Likewise, if there are disagreements within a group over proposed legislation, congressional actors see this as evidence of a rocky road to passage. Consciously or unconsciously, when a government group (particularly the NGA) can't come to agreement on an issue, it is taking on an obstructor role for that legislation. Time and time again, respondents said that if the governors were not satisfied with a proposal, that proposal had slim chances of passage.

The government groups are experiencing a period of change in their relationship with the federal government. They are not able to gain increased federal grants the way they once were, nor are they viewed as negatively as they were under the Reagan administration. The groups must fight to retain some programs that were once sacrosanct, but their views are nonetheless important when Congress is developing or expanding programs that will be implemented at the subnational level. If the state and local interest groups are to learn any lesson from the legislation considered in this study, it is to take advantage of a window of opportunity when it exists. The NGA did this with welfare reform in 1988, when they lobbied for a significant expansion of an existing grant program. The opportunity to expand the grant system has passed. The NGA and the other government groups see in 1995 an opportunity to increase their authority over programs, but are hesitant to seize the opportunity when it means limiting the dollar amount of federal grants to the states. Regardless of what phase of intergovernmental lobbying the groups are in, states and localities always wish for more money with fewer strings attached. Most of the fourth phase has been characterized by less money and, until recently, more strings. That may be changing, as conservatives in Congress see an opportunity of decentralizing social programs and spending less money on them. If decentralization means fewer strings, state and local groups will be happy, perhaps moving us into a fifth phase of intergovernmental lobbying. But if fewer strings are attached to less money, state and local groups will have a difficult time achieving the consensus necessary for lobbying success.

NOTES

1. Haider, *When Governments Come to Washington*, pp. 48–75.

2. Hays, "Intergovernmental Lobbying," p. 1085. The NGA testified 412 times between 1979 and 1989, more times than any other state and local group. (NACO came in second, testifying 350 times.) The NGA's budget was $8,300,000 in 1988. Again, NACO's budget was the next highest, at $8 million.

3. Berry, *Lobbying for the People*.

4. See Jeffrey L. Katz, "Governors Sidelined in Welfare Debate, *Congressional Quarterly Weekly Report*, May 20, 1995, pp. 1423–1425.

Appendix I

Interview Guide for Congressional Staff

This interview is part of a study of the influence of state and local government interest groups on congressional legislation. The study will examine the role of the state and local groups in the passage of three bills: the Family Support Act, the Act for Better Childcare Services and the Cranston-Gonzalez National Affordable Housing Act. The questions you will be asked will focus on [NAME, YEAR OF ACT] and the role of interest groups at various stages in the legislative process. The same questions will be asked of majority and minority staff in Congress who worked on each of the three acts; similar questions will be asked of state and local interest group staff.

1. Thinking back to when [NAME, YEAR OF ACT] was first introduced in Congress, was there any particular individual, group or event that placed [WELFARE, CHILD CARE, HOUSING] on the congressional agenda? (This includes *all* interest groups, not just state and local groups.) Please explain. Were there any other individuals, groups or events that were instrumental in placing [WELFARE, CHILD CARE, HOUSING] on the agenda? [IF STATE/LOCAL GROUPS HAVEN'T BEEN MENTIONED: Did the state and local interest groups play a role?] How important was each individual's, group's or event's role?

2. Were any outside groups or individuals involved in drafting the legislation? What groups or individuals? In what way were they involved (i.e., technical assistance/background information, interest groups wrote portions of the legislation, or the legislation was written with interest groups in mind)? Did representatives of states and localities play a role at this stage of the process? Please describe.

3. After [NAME, YEAR OF ACT] was introduced, what role did state and local interest groups play as the act was being considered in committee or subcommittee? What particular provisions of this legislation were state and local interest groups concerned with? What other groups were concerned with these provisions? Were their views similar to or opposite of state and local views?

4. Aside from testimony at congressional hearings, how did state and local groups make known their position on particular provisions/issues? For example, did interest group staff confer with congressional staff or did interest group members (such as governors) contact congressional staff or members of Congress? What effect did this have on these provisions?

5. Was there any provision in the legislation in which state and local groups were particularly influential? Please explain.

6. Was there any provision or issue on which state and local groups took a strong position, but were ultimately unsuccessful? What was the provision or issue? Why do you believe they were unsuccessful?

7. Did state and local interest groups act in a coalition with each other and/or with other groups? Which, if any, groups formed coalitions? What was their common interest? What effect did coalitions have on the process?

8. Overall, what interest groups do you believe were most influential in passage of this legislation? [PROBE: Were there any other outside groups or individuals that were influential?] Now, I'm going to read back to you the names of the groups (or individuals) that you have just mentioned, plus some other groups that may have been involved in the legislation. As I read the list, please rate the overall impact of each group (or individual) on a scale of 1 to 10, with 1 representing a very low impact and 10 a very high impact.

9. I'm going to read the list of groups (or individuals) again. During the time legislation was considered by your committee, how often were you contacted by the groups just mentioned? Daily, weekly, monthly?

10. Overall, how important were *state and local groups* in passage of *this legislation*? Please rate the overall impact of each of these groups on a scale of 1 to 10.

1	2	3	4	5	6	7	8	9	10
Low impact								High	Impact

National Governors' Association
National Conference of State Legislatures
U.S. Conference of Mayors
National Association of Counties
National League of Cities

11. How does the final legislation compare with the desires of the state and local groups at the beginning of the process? Do you believe the state/local groups got legislation consistent with their initial preferences?

12. Did the media cover [NAME, YEAR OF ACT] as it was being considered in Congress? Did this coverage include attention to state and local lobbies?

13. Are you aware of any other recently enacted national legislation in which state and local groups played a significant role? How did their role in that legislation compare with their role in [NAME OF ACT]? Would you say the state and local groups were more or less influential on [NAME OF ACT] than on other legislation?

14. *In general,* how would you characterize the attitudes of congressional staff toward state and local interest groups? On a scale of 1 to 10, 1 being very unfavorable and 10 being very favorable, where would you place the attitudes of congressional staff toward state and local groups? Use the same scale to rank the attitudes of members of Congress. How do congressional attitudes toward state and local interest groups compare to attitudes toward other interest groups?

1	2	3	4	5	6	7	8	9	10
Unfavorable								Favorable	

National Governors' Association
National Conference of State Legislatures
U.S. Conference of Mayors
National Association of Counties
National League of Cities

15. Please rank state and local interest groups in terms of their *general influence* in Congress in the issue areas with which you are familiar. Use a scale of 1 to 10, 1 being very low influence, 10 being very influential.

1	2	3	4	5	6	7	8	9	10
Very low influence								Very influential	

   National Governors' Association
   National Conference of State Legislatures
   U.S. Conference of Mayors
   National Association of Counties
   National League of Cities

16. *In general*, how often are you contacted by state and local interest groups?

	Daily	Weekly	Monthly	Yearly
National Governors' Association				
National Conference of State Legislatures				
National Association of Counties				
U.S. Conference of Mayors				
National League of Cities				

17. Now, I'd like to get some background information. What is your official title? What issue areas do you focus on? How long have you been working in this office?

Appendix 2

Interview Guide for Association Staff

This interview is part of a study of the influence of state and local government interest groups on congressional legislation. The study will examine the role of the state and local groups in the passage of congressional legislation by focusing on three bills: the Family Support Act, the Act for Better Child Care and the Cranston-Gonzalez National Affordable Housing Act. The questions you will be asked will focus on [NAME, YEAR OF ACT] and the role of your organization at various stages of the legislative process. Similar questions will be asked of congressional staff and staff of other state and local interest groups.

1. Thinking back to when [NAME, YEAR OF ACT] was first introduced in Congress, was there any particular individual, group or event that placed [WELFARE, CHILD CARE, HOUSING] on the congressional agenda? Do you feel that your group played a role in bringing [WELFARE, CHILD CARE, HOUSING] to national attention? In what way?

2. At the time the legislation was originally introduced, what were your group's major concerns in the area of [WELFARE, CHILD CARE, HOUSING]?

3. Was your group involved in drafting the legislation? In what way (i.e., technical assistance/background information, your group actually wrote portions of the legislation)?

4. What other groups were involved with [NAME, YEAR OF ACT]? Were these groups in agreement with or in opposition to your position on the act? Did your group act in a coalition with other state/local interest groups? Which groups? Did one of the interest groups take a "lead" role in this coalition?

Which one? Were there other coalitions involved in this legislation? What groups did they consist of?

5.   After [NAME, YEAR OF ACT] was introduced, what particular provisions was your group concerned with? Were there any conflicts between your group and other groups over these or other provisions/issues?

6.   How did your group decide its position on particular issues (for example, through general staff meetings and surveys of members or through hierarchical channels such as committee meetings)? Was there any conflict within the group on any issues? Please explain.

7.   How did your group make known to Congress its position on particular provisions/issues? For example, did your staff confer with congressional staff or did your group members contact congressional staff or Members of Congress? What kind of reception do you feel your staff got in Congress? (That is, how willing were congressional staff to meet with and/or talk to your staff?) What kind of reception do you feel your group members got in Congress?

8.   Did the media (print or broadcast) cover [NAME, YEAR OF ACT] and its passage through Congress? Did the media cover your group's or other state or local interest group's role in consideration of the legislation? Did your group actively seek media attention on this act? In what ways (for example, press conferences, press releases, paid advertising)?

9.   Was there any provision in the legislation on which you feel your group was particularly successful? Please explain.

10. Was there any provision or issue on which your group took a strong position, but was ultimately unsuccessful? What was the provision/issue? Why do you believe you were not successful?

11. Overall, what impact do you think your organization had on this legislation? How would this compare to the impact of other interest groups?

12. What interest groups do you believe were most influential in passage of this legislation? [PROBE: Were there any other outside groups or individuals that were influential?] Now, I'm going to read back to you the names of the groups (or individuals) that you have just mentioned, plus some other groups that may have been involved in the legislation. As I read the list, please rate the overall impact of each group (or individual) on a scale of 1 to 10, with 1 representing a very low impact and 10 a very high impact.

13. How does the final legislation compare with the desires of your group at the beginning of the process? Do you think the legislation is consistent with your group's initial preferences? Is the legislation consistent with the preferences of other interest groups? Which ones?

14. Listed on this card are some of the final provisions of the act over which there was some conflict during consideration in Congress. Please rate the consistency of these provisions to your group's initial position on a scale of 1 to 10.

1	2	3	4	5	6	7	8	9	10
Inconsistent								Very consistent	

CHILD CARE
   National Standards
   Grant Program
   Vouchers
   Local Issues
   Tax Credits
   Administrative Costs
HOUSING
   Home block grants
   CDBG
   Matching grants
   HOPE subsidies to help poor families buy apartments
   Funding level
WELFARE REFORM
   Minimum benefits
   Participation rates
   Mandatory work
   Child support enforcement
   AFDC-UP
   Funding Match
   Transitional Benefits

15. Has your organization been significantly involved in other recently enacted ntional legislation? What legislation? How did your group's success in that legislation compare with your group's success in [NAME OF ACT]?

16. *In general*, how would you characterize the attitudes of congressional staff toward your organization and other state and local interest groups? On a scale of 1 to 10, 1 being very unfavorable and 10 being very favorable, where would

you place the attitudes of congressional staff toward your organization and other state and local groups? [HAND CARD] Use the same scale to rank the attitudes of Members of Congress. How do congressional attitudes toward state and local interest groups compare to attitudes toward other interest groups?

1	2	3	4	5	6	7	8	9	10
Very Unfavorable								Very Favorable	

National Governors' Association
National Conference of State Legislatures
U.S. Conference of Mayors
National Association of Counties
National League of Cities

17. Please rank state and local interest groups in terms of their *general influence* in Congress in the issue areas with which you are familiar. Use a scale of 1 to 10, 1 being very low influence, 10 being very influential.

1	2	3	4	5	6	7	8	9	10
Very low influence								Very influential	

National Governors' Association
National Conference of State Legislatures
U.S. Conference of Mayors
National Association of Counties
National League of Cities

18. Since passage of [NAME OF ACT], has your organization attempted to monitor its implementation? In what ways? Has your organization contacted an appropriations subcommittee about the funding for the act? Has your organization contacted the executive branch about the regulations regarding the implementation of the act?

19. Now, I'd like to get some background information. What is your official title? How long have you been working for this organization?

Bibliography

PRIMARY SOURCES

Congressional Hearings

U.S. Congress. House. Committee on Banking, Finance and Urban Affairs. *Urgent Relief for the Homeless Act. Hearings before the Subcommittee on Housing and Community Development.* 100th Cong., 1st sess., 1987.

U.S. Congress. House. Committee on Banking, Finance and Urban Affairs. *CDBG and UDAG Displacement. Hearing before the Subcommittee on Housing and Community Development.* 100th Cong., 2nd sess., 1988.

U.S. Congress. House. Committee on Banking, Finance and Urban Affairs. *Developing a National Housing Policy. Field Hearing before the Subcommittee on Housing and Community Development.* 100th Cong., 2nd sess., 1988 (Trenton, New Jersey).

U.S. Congress. House. Committee on Banking, Finance and Urban Affairs. *State Housing Initiatives and the Role of the Federal Government. Hearing before the Subcommittee on Housing and Community Development.* 100th Cong., 2nd sess., 1988.

U.S. Congress. House. Committee on Banking, Finance and Urban Affairs. *Housing and Community Development Act of 1989. Hearings before the Subcommittee on Housing and Community Development.* 101st Cong., 1st sess., 1989.

U.S. Congress. House. Committee on Education and Labor. *Hearings on Welfare Reform: H. R. 30, Fair Work Opportunities Act of 1970 and H. R. 1720, Family Welfare Reform Act of 1987.* 100th Cong., 1st sess. 1987.

U.S. Congress. House. Committee on Education and Labor. *H. R. 3660, The Act for Better Child Care. Hearings Before the Subcommittee on Human*

Resources. 100th Cong. , 2nd sess., 1988.

U.S. Congress. House. Committee on Ways and Means. *Work, Education and Training Opportunities for Welfare Recipients. Hearings before the Subcommittee on Public Assistance and Unemployment Compensation.* 99th Cong., 2nd sess., 1986.

U.S. Congress. House. Committee on Ways and Means. *Family Welfare Reform Act. Hearings before the Subcommittee on Public Assistance and Unemployment Compensation.* 100th Cong., 1st sess., 1987.

U.S. Congress. House. Committee on Ways and Means. *The Act for Better Child Care. Hearings before the Subcommittee on Human Resources.* 100th Cong., 2nd sess., 1988.

U.S. Congress. Senate. Committee on Banking, Housing and Urban Affairs. *Homelessness in America. Hearings before the Subcommittee on Housing and Urban Affairs.* 100th Cong., 1st sess., 1987.

U.S. Congress. Senate. Committee on Banking, Housing and Urban Affairs. *The National Affordable Housing Act. Hearings before the Subcommittee on Housing and Urban Affairs.* 100th Cong., 2nd sess., 1988.

U.S. Congress. Senate. Committee on Banking, Housing and Urban Affairs. *The Role of State and Local Governments Developing Strategies with Emphasis on S. 566. Hearings before the Subcommittee on Housing and Urban Affairs.* 101st Cong., 1st sess., 1989.

U.S. Congress. Senate. Committee on Banking, Housing and Urban Affairs. *The "Homeownership and Opportunity for People Everywhere" [HOPE] Initiatives. Joint Hearings before the Committee and the Subcommittee on Housing and Urban Affairs.* 101st Cong., 2nd sess., 1990.

U.S. Congress. Senate. Committee on Finance. *Welfare Reform or Replacement (Child Support Enforcement). Hearing before the Subcommittee on Social Security and Family Policy.* 100th Cong., 1st sess., 1987.

U.S. Congress. Senate. Committee on Finance. *Welfare Reform or Replacement (Child Support Enforcement II). Hearing before the Subcommittee on Social Security and Family Policy.* 100th Cong., 1st sess., 1987.

U.S. Congress. Senate. Committee on Finance. *Welfare Reform or Replacement (Short Term vs. Long Term Dependency). Hearing before the Subcommittee on Social Security and Family Policy.* 100th Cong., 1st sess., 1987.

U.S. Congress. Senate. Committee on Finance. *Welfare Reform or Replacement (Work and Welfare). Hearing before the Subcommittee on Social Security and Family Policy.* 100th Cong., 1st sess., 1987.

U.S. Congress. Senate. Committee on Labor and Human Resources. *S. 1885, the Act for Better Child Care Services of 1987.* 100th Cong., 1st sess., 1987.

U.S. Congress. Senate Committee on Labor and Human Resources. *Smart Start: The Community Collaboration for Early Childhood Development Act of 1988. Hearings.* 100th Cong., 2nd sess., 1988.

Association Documents

American Public Welfare Association. *Case Management and Welfare Reform*. Washington: American Public Welfare Association, July 31, 1987.

National Association of Counties. *Highlights, HOME Investment Partnerships Act*. Washington: National Association of Counties, July 1987.

―――. *Proposal for a New National Housing Policy*. Submitted to the Subcommittee on Housing of the Senate Committee on Banking, Housing and Urban Affairs. Washington: National Association of Counties, 1987.

―――. "The 100th Congress and NACO." *County News* 20 (November 1988): Sec. B. Washington: National Association of Counties.

―――. *Get Involved in the Job Opportunities and Basic Skills Training Program: What Local Areas Need to Know*. Washington: National Association of Counties, 1989.

―――. "101st Congress Issues Wrap-Up." *County News* 22 (November 1990): Sec. B. Washington: National Association of Counties.

―――. *Community and Economic Development* (Policy Statement). Washington: National Association of Counties, 1991.

National Conference of State Legislatures. *A Comparison of Child Care Legislation in Conference Committee before the 101st Congress*. Washington: National Conference of State Legislatures, October 1989.

―――. *Child Care and Early Education Policy: A Legislator's Guide*. Denver: National Conference of State Legislatures, 1990.

―――. *1989 State Legislative Summary: Children, Youth and Family Issues*. Denver: National Conference of State Legislatures, 1990.

―――. *101st Congress in Review. Child Care: A Summary and Analysis of New Federal Programs and Tax Credits*. Denver: National Conference of State Legislatures, 1990.

―――. *Action Alert: Child Care Conference to Begin*. Washington: National Conference of State Legislatures, 1990.

―――. *State-Federal Issue Brief: Summary of the 101st Congress, Second Session*. Denver: National Conference of State Legislatures, 1990.

―――. *Official Policy. Human Services. Child Care*. Washington: National Conference of State Legislatures, undated.

National Council of State Housing Agencies. *Comparison of Senate and House Omnibus Housing Legislation, S 566 and HR 1180*. Washington: National Council of State Housing Agencies, 1989.

National Governors' Association. *A Governor's Guide to the Family Support Act: Challenges and Opportunities*. Washington: National Governors' Association.

―――. *Governors' Weekly Bulletin*. Washington: National Governors' Association, 1990.

―――. *NGA Priority Issues*. Washington: National Governors' Association, 1990.

————. *Taxing Care: State Developments in Child Care*. Washington: National Governors' Association, 1990.

————. *Washington Representatives: Memoranda*. Washington: National Governors' Association, 1990.

National League of Cities. *1991 National Municipal Policy*. Washington: National League of Cities, 1991.

U.S. Conference of Mayors. *U.S. Mayor* 58 (July 1991). Washington: U.S. Conference of Mayors.

Newspaper Articles

Anderson, Jack, and Van Atta, Dale. "Time for New Ideas on Child Care." *Washington Post*, July 16, 1989, sec. B, p. 7.

Berke, Richard L. "Dukakis Says He Would Commit $3 Billion to Build New Housing." *New York Times*, June 29, 1988.

"Billions in U.S. Aid Urged for Low-Income Homes." *New York Times*, March 29, 1988, sec. B, p. 20.

Blakely, Steve. "Local Officials Gird for Fight over Federal Aid." *Congressional Quarterly Weekly Report*, January 25, 1987, p. 168.

Broder, David. "Governors Endorse Welfare Overhaul." *Washington Post*, February 25, 1987, sec. A, p. 3.

Clinton, Bill. "Welfare Reform as an Investment." *Washington Post*, December 10, 1987, sec. A, p. 27.

Dewar, Helen. "As Debate on Child Care Opens, Senators Agree on Goal but Diverge on Means." *Washington Post*, June 16, 1989, sec. A, p. 8.

Edelman, Marian Wright. "Pass That Child Care Bill." *Washington Post*, June 20, 1989, sec. A, p. 23.

Heineman, Ben W., Jr. "Time for Welfare Reform: Everyone Agrees Work Is the Answer, but What's the Question?" *Washington Post*, February 15, 1987, sec. C, p. 2.

Ifill, Gwen. "City Leaders Decry Lack of Affordable Housing." *Washington Post*, January 13, 1989, sec. A, p. 7.

Katz, Jeffrey L. "Governors Sidelined in Welfare Debate." *Congressional Quarterly Weekly Report*, May 20, 1995, pp. 1423–1425.

Knudsen, Patrick L. "After Long, Bruising Battle, House Approves Welfare Bill." *Congressional Quarterly Weekly Report*, December 19, 1987, p. 3157.

————. "Committees Starting to Focus on Child Care." *Congressional Quarterly Weekly Report*, February 27, 1988, pp. 514–515.

Kuntz, Phil. "Expiring Federal Subsidies Raise a Policy Dilemma." *Congressional Quarterly Weekly Report*, May 6, 1989, pp. 1041–1045.

————., and Biskupic, Joan. "New Investigations Launched as HUD Scandal Widens." *Congressional Quarterly Weekly Report*, June 17, 1989, p. 1477.

Mann, Judy. "Childish Performance on the Child Care Bill." *Washington Post*, November 22, 1989, sec. B, p. 3.

Mariano, Ann. "Who Will Get Government Housing Aid?" *Washington Post*, January 28, 1989, sec. F, pp. 1, 2.

—————. "New Congress, Bush to Face Housing Crisis." *Washington Post*, January 14, 1989, sec. E, pp. 1, 8.

May, Clifford D. "Kemp Puts Focus on Urban Change." *New York Times*, June 20, 1989, sec. B, p. 6.

Pear, Robert. "Sweeping Welfare Revision Plan Stresses Responsibility of Parents." *New York Times*, July 19, 1987.

Rich, Spencer. "Reagan Welfare Proposal Criticized by Agencies." *Washington Post*, February 10, 1987, sec. A, p. 8.

—————. "Child Care, Housing Listed as Top Urban Priorities." *Washington Post*, August 29, 1989, sec. A, p. 3.

Rovner, Julie. "Governors Jump-Start Welfare Reform Drive." *Congressional Quarterly Weekly Report*, February 28, 1987, p. 376.

—————. "Reagan Team Tears into Democrats' Welfare Plan." *Congressional Quarterly Weekly Report*, April 4, 1987, p. 627.

—————. "Welfare Reform: The Next Domestic Priority?" *Congressional Quarterly Weekly Report*, September 27, 1987, p. 2281.

—————. "Governors Press Reagan, Bentsen on Welfare." *Congressional Quarterly Weekly Report*, February 27, 1988, p. 512.

—————. "Deep Schisms Still Imperil Welfare Overhaul." *Congressional Quarterly Weekly Report*, June 18, 1988, p. 1650.

—————. "Day Care Package Clears First Hurdle in the House." *Congressional Quarterly Weekly Report*, July 2, 1988, pp. 1833-1836.

—————. "Both Parties Seek to Patch Gaps in Their Image. *Congressional Quarterly Weekly Report*, July 30, 1988, p. 2076.

—————. "Welfare Conferees Narrow Their Differences." *Congressional Quarterly Weekly Report*, August 6, 1988, p. 2202.

—————. "Congress Clears Overhaul of Welfare System." *Congressional Quarterly Weekly Report*, October 1, 1988, p. 2202.

—————. "Congress Approves Overhaul of Welfare System." *Congressional Quarterly Weekly Report*, October 8, 1988, pp. 2825-2831.

—————. "Congress Shifts Its Attention to the Working Poor." *Congressional Quarterly Weekly Report*, February 18, 1989, pp. 326-328.

—————. "Child Care Debate Intensifies as ABC Bill Is Approved." *Congressional Quarterly Weekly Report*, March 18, 1989, p. 587.

—————. "Draft Welfare Regulations Draw Fire from the States." *Congressional Quarterly Weekly Report*, May 20, 1989, pp. 1191-1194.

—————. "Panel Approves Child Care Bill after Rancorous Markup." *Congressional Quarterly Weekly Report*, July 1, 1989, pp. 1629-1631.

—————. "House Child Care Proposals Survive Floor Challenges."

Congressional Quarterly Weekly Report, October 7, 1989, pp. 2639-2640.

————. House-Senate Conferees Agree on New Child Care Program."
Congressional Quarterly Weekly Report, November 11, 1989, p. 3070.

————. "Delay on Child Care Measure Prompts Angry Criticism."
Congressional Quarterly Weekly Report, November 18, 1989, p. 3162.

————. "Long Deadlock on Child Care May Get Resolved Soon."
Congressional Quarterly Weekly Report, March 10, 1990, p. 751.

————. "Church-State Squabble Stalls Child Care Bill in House."
Congressional Quarterly Weekly Report, March 24, 1990, pp. 920–921.

————. "Bush Veto Threat Shadows Child Care Legislation." *Congressional
Quarterly Weekly Report*, March 31, 1990, pp. 998–1001.

Toner, Robin. "Senate Gets Housing Measure Aimed at Keeping Costs Low."
New York Times, March 16, 1989, sec. A.

"Welfare Reform: Big Proposals, Small Fixes." *Congressional Quarterly Weekly
Report*, September 27, 1986, p. 2285.

Yoder, Edwin M., Jr. "Listen to Moynihan on Kids in Poverty." *Washington
Post*, July 29, 1987, sec. A, p. 15.

Zuckman, Jill. "Conferees' Authorization Bill Marks Turnabout in Policy."
Congressional Quarterly Weekly Report, October 20, 1990, p. 3514.

Other

Advisory Commission on Intergovernmental Relations. *Significant Features of
Fiscal Federalism*. 2 vols. Washington: U.S. Government Printing Office,
October 1991.

Task Force on Poverty and Welfare. New York State. *A New Social Contract:
Rethinking the Nature and Purpose of Public Assistance*. Albany: Executive
Chamber, Task Force on Poverty and Welfare, 1986.

U.S. Congress. House. Democratic Caucus. "The Road to Independence:
Strengthening America's Families in Need." Washington: House Democratic
Caucus, July 30, 1986.

U.S. Congress. *Family Support Act of 1988: Conference Report*. Number 100-
998. Washington: U.S. Government Printing Office, 1989.

SECONDARY SOURCES

Allison, Graham T. *Essence of Decision: Explaining the Cuban Missile Crisis*.
Boston: Little, Brown and Co., 1971.

Bauer, Raymond A., de Sola Pool, Ithiel, and Dexter, Lewis Anthony. *American
Business and Public Policy*. Chicago: Aldine-Atherton, Inc., 1972.

Baum, Erica. "When the Witch Doctors Agree: The Family Support Act and

Social Science Research." *Journal of Policy Analysis and Management* 10 (1991): 603–615.

Beer, Samuel H. "Federalism, Nationalism and Democracy in America." *American Political Science Review* 72 (1978): 9-21.

Berry, Jeffrey. *The Interest Group Society*. Boston: Little, Brown and Co., 1984.

———. *Lobbying for the People*. Princeton: Princeton University Press, 1977.

Brodkin, Evelyn Z. *The False Promise of Administrative Reform: Implementing Quality Control in Welfare*. Philadelphia: Temple University Press, 1986.

Browne, William P. "Organized Interests and Their Issue Niches: A Search for Pluralism in a Policy Domain." *Journal of Politics* 52 (May 1990): 477–509.

Campbell, Donald T., and Stanley, Julian C. *Experimental and Quasi-Experimental Designs for Research*. Boston: Houghton-Mifflin Co., 1963.

Cigler, Allan, and Loomis, Burdett A., ed. *Interest Group Politics*, 2nd ed. Washington: Congressional Quarterly Press, 1986.

———. "Organized Interests and the Search for Certainty." In *Interest Group Politics*, 2nd ed., chapter 18. Edited by Allan Cigler and Burdett A. Loomis. Washington: Congressional Quarterly Press, 1986.

Clark, Peter B., and Wilson, James Q. "Incentive Systems: A Theory of Organizations." *Administrative Science Quarterly* 6 (September 1961): 129-166.

Conlan, Timothy. *New Federalism: Intergovernmental Reform from Nixon to Reagan*. Washington: The Brookings Institution, 1988.

Dahl, Robert A. *Who Governs? Democracy and Power in an American City*. New Haven: Yale University Press, 1961.

Danziger, Sheldon, and Weinberg, David. *Fighting Poverty, What Works and What Doesn't*. Cambridge, Mass.: Harvard University Press, 1986.

Day, Christine L. *What Older Americans Think*. Princeton: Princeton University Press, 1990.

Derthick, Martha, and Quirk, Paul. *The Politics of Deregulation*. Washington: The Brookings Institution, 1985.

Dexter, Lewis Anthony. *How Organizations are Represented in Washington*. Indianapolis: The Bobbs-Merrill Co., Inc., 1969.

Eisinger, Peter, and Gormley, William, eds. *The Midwest Response to the New Federalism*. Madison: University of Wisconsin Press, 1988.

Evans, Diana M. "Lobbying the Committee: Interest Groups and the House Public Works and Transportation Committee." In Allan Cigler and Burdett A. Loomis, ed. *Interest Group Politics*, 2nd ed., chapter 12. Washington: Congressional Quarterly Press, 1986.

Farkas, Suzanne. *Urban Lobbying: Mayors in the Federal Arena*. New York: New York University Press, 1971.

Feagin, Joe R., Orum, Anthony M., and Sjoberg, Gideon, ed. *A Case for the Case Study*. Chapel Hill: University of North Carolina Press, 1991.

Gelb, Joyce, and Palley, Marian Lief. *Women and Public Policies*. Princeton:

Princeton University Press, 1987.

Gormley, William. *The Politics of Public Utility Regulation*. Pittsburgh: University of Pittsburgh Press, 1983.

Greenwald, Carol S. *Group Power, Lobbying and Public Policy*. New York: Praeger Publishers, 1977.

Gueron, Judith. *Reforming Welfare with Work, Occasional Paper 2*. New York: Ford Foundation Project on Social Welfare and the American Future, 1987.

Haider, Donald. *When Governments Come to Washington: Governors, Mayors and Intergovernmental Lobbying*. New York: The Free Press, 1974.

Haskins, Ron. "Congress Writes a Law: Research and Welfare Reform." *Journal of Policy Analysis and Management* 10 (1991): 616-632.

Hayes, Michael T. *Lobbyists and Legislators*. New Brunswick, N.J.: Rutgers University Press, 1981.

—————. "The Semi-Sovereign Pressure Groups: A Critique of Current Theory and an Alternative Typology." *Journal of Politics* 40 (1978): 136-161.

Hays, R. Allen. "Intergovernmental Lobbying: Toward an Understanding of Priorities." *Western Political Quarterly* 44 (December 1991): 1081-1098.

Heclo, Hugh. "Issue Networks and the Executive Establishment." In Anthony King, ed., *The New American Political System*, 2nd ed., chapter 3. Washington: American Enterprise Institute for Public Policy Research, 1978.

Kingdon, John. *Agendas, Alternatives and Public Policies*. New York: HarperCollins College Publishers, 1995.

Knoke, David. *Organizing for Collective Action: the Political Economies of Association*. New York: Aldine De Gruyter, 1990.

Levine, Charles H., and Thurber, James A. "Reagan and the Intergovernmental Lobby: Iron Triangles, Cozy Subsystems and Political Conflict." In Allan Cigler and Burdett A. Loomis, ed., *Interest Group Politics*, 2nd ed., pp. 202-220. Washington: Congressional Quarterly Press, 1986.

Lowi, Theodore. "American Business, Public Policy, Case Studies and Political Theory." *World Politics* 16 (July 1964): 677-715.

—————. *The End of Liberalism*. New York: W.W. Norton & Co., 1979.

McFarland, Andrew. *Public Interest Lobbies: Decision-Making on Energy*. Washington: American Enterprise Institute for Public Policy Research, 1976.

Milbrath, Lester W. *The Washington Lobbyists*. Chicago: Rand McNally & Co., 1963.

Moynihan, Daniel Patrick. *The Politics of a Guaranteed Income: The Nixon Administration and the Family Assistance Plan*. New York: Random House, 1973.

Murphy, Jerome T. *Getting the Facts: A Fieldwork Guide for Evaluators and Policy Analysts*. Santa Monica: Goodyear Publishing Co., Inc., 1980.

Murray, Charles. *Losing Ground: American Social Policy 1950-1980*. New York: Basic Books, 1984.

Nightingale, Demetra. *Evaluation of the Massachusetts Employment and*

Training Choices Program. Washington: The Urban Institute, 1990.

Novak, Michael, et al. *The New Consensus on Family and Welfare: A Community of Self-Reliance*. Washington: American Enterprise Institute for Public Policy Research, 1987.

Olson, Mancur, Jr. *The Logic of Collective Action*. New York: Schocken Books, 1970.

O'Neill, June. *Work and Welfare in Massachusetts: An Evaluation of the ET Program*. Boston: Pioneer Institute for Public Policy Research, 1990.

Peterson, Paul. *City Limits*. Chicago: University of Chicago Press, 1981.

Piven, Frances Fox, and Cloward, Richard A. *Poor People's Movements: Why They Succeed, How They Fail*. New York: Pantheon Books, 1977.

Reed, B. J. "The Changing Role of Local Advocacy in National Politics." *Journal of Urban Affairs* 5 (1983): 287–298.

Ripley, Randall, and Franklin, Grace A. *Congress, the Bureaucracy and Public Policy*. Homewood, Ill.: The Dorsey Press, 1984.

Sabato, Larry. *Goodbye to Good-time Charlie*. Washington: Congressional Quarterly Press, 1983.

Salisbury, Robert. "An Exchange Theory of Interest Groups." *Midwest Journal of Political Science* 13 (February 1969): 1-31.

Schattschneider, E. E. *The Semisovereign People*. New York: Holt, Rinehart and Winston, 1960.

Schram, Sanford F. "The New Federalism and Social Welfare: AFDC in the Midwest." In *The Midwest Response to the New Federalism*, pp. 264-292. Edited by Peter Eisinger and William Gormley. Madison: University of Wisconsin Press, 1988.

Schwarz, John. *America's Hidden Success: A Reassessment of Public Policy from Kennedy to Reagan*. New York: W.W. Norton and Co., 1988.

Sjoberg, Gideon; Williams, Norma; Vaughan, Ted and Sjoberg, Andree F. "The Case Study Approach in Social Research: Basic Methodological Issues." In *A Case for the Case Study*, chapter 1. Edited by Joe R. Feagin, Anthony Drum and Gideon Sjoberg. Chapel Hill: University of North Carolina Press, 1991.

Skocpol, Theda. *Social Policy in the United States: Future Possibilities in Historical Perspective*. Princeton: Princeton University Press, 1995.

Stone, Clarence. *Regime Politics: Governing Atlanta, 1946-1988*. Lawrence: University Press of Kansas, 1989.

Truman, David. *The Governmental Process*. New York: Knopf, 1951.

Walker, Jack. "Origins and Maintenance of Interest Groups." *American Political Science Review* 77 (1983): 390–406.

Wilson, James Q. *American Government: Institutions and Policies*, 3rd ed. Lexington, Mass.: D.C. Heath and Company, 1986.

Wootton, Graham. *Interest Groups: Policy and Politics in America*. Englewood Cliffs, N.J.: Prentice-Hall, 1985.

Yin, Robert K. *Case Study Research: Design and Methods*. Beverly Hills: Sage, 1984.

Zeigler, L. Harmon. *Interest Groups in American Society*. Englewood Cliffs, N.J.: Prentice-Hall, 1964.

Index

About the Author

ANNE MARIE CAMMISA is Assistant Professor of Government at Suffolk University in Boston, and during 1993–1994, was an American Political Science Association Congressional Fellow. She holds degrees from the University of Virginia and Georgetown University.

ISBN 0-275-94962-1

EAN

HARDCOVER BAR CODE